CAN'T SIT STILL

The Adventurous Life of an
Immigrant Entrepreneur

By James Kamstra

Kamstra Ecostudies

CAN'T SIT STILL:
THE ADVENTUROUS LIFE OF AN IMMIGRANT ENTREPRENEUR
Copyright © James Kamstra 2021

All rights reserved. No part of this book may be used or reproduced by any means, graphic, electronic, or mechanical, including photocopying, recording, taping, or by any information storage retrieval system without the written permission of the author except in the case of brief quotations embodied in critical articles and reviews. For permission, please contact the author at hoakamstra@gmail.com.

ISBN 978-1-7776247-0-5 – book
ISBN 978-1-7776247-1-2 – hardcover book
978-1-7776247-2-9 – electronic book

Cover Design: Design Pickle
Interior Design: Words and More
Editing: Jackie Brown Books

DEDICATION

To My Mother

Cornelia Maria Kamstra

TABLE OF CONTENTS

Foreword
Prologue
Chapter 1: From Where He Came 1
Chapter 2: World War II and German Occupation 10
Chapter 3: Coming of Age in Peacetime 20
Chapter 4: Leaving the Netherlands 31
Chapter 5: Taking a New Name in Nova Scotia 35
Chapter 6: Ontario, the Place to Be 41
Chapter 7: Woman of His Dreams 45
Chapter 8: Time to Start a Family 51
Chapter 9: Landscaping — A New Career 59
Chapter 10: Partnership with Rundle 64
Chapter 11: Striking Out with his Own Business 72
Chapter 12: Moving it All to Taunton 79
Chapter 13: Leisure Time and Family Vacations 86
Chapter 14: Paddle Forth 97
Chapter 15: The Kids in Their Teenage Years 104
Chapter 16: Inviting Brother Sid into the Business 113
Chapter 17: Sons in the Business 116
Chapter 18: If It's Not from Kamstra, It's Just Dirt 127
Chapter 19: Well Water with Fizz 132
Chapter 20: Students from the Netherlands 134
Chapter 21: Social and Service Clubs 138
Chapter 22: Meddling in Real Estate 148
Chapter 23: The Sky Beckons 153
Chapter 24: A Mexican Business Venture 168
Chapter 25: Hook, Line, and Sinker 171
Chapter 26: Accidents Will Happen 181
Chapter 27: Should have Left Well Enough Alone 187
Chapter 28: A Menagerie of Animals 190
Chapter 29: Exotic Travels in the 1980s and Beyond 186
Chapter 30: One More Dream Home 210
Chapter 31: A Stroke of Bad Luck 214
Chapter 32: A Reflection of the Man 221

Foreword

I wrote this book to preserve the memory of my father's life. Jim was a dynamic driven man with a sense of purpose, who left an impression on many people that he met. He was a pillar of his family, a helpful friend to many, but he had his own agenda which created conflicts along the way. I think the title "Can't Sit Still", captures the kind of person that Jim was. Always on the go, always doing something, he could never sit back and relax for long.

I have tried to depict a chronology of his life, recording major milestones, accomplishments, and turning points. I have also described numerous small happenings that took place over his lifetime, some humorous, some adventurous, some serious, and some not very flattering. I have tried to show what drove him as well as the different relationships he had with people, either as a son, brother, husband, father, boss, business partner, fishing buddy, or as a stranger willing to help someone in need. Of course, it is not possible for a book to cover all, or even most of the many happenings over a person's long lifetime. What is portrayed is a collection of events that show a cross-section of someone who lived a full life.

I acquired much of the material for this book through a series of interviews with Jim, conducted while he was in hospital after his stroke in 2015. More material came from my personal memories of my dad as well as from notes in diaries and field books that I had written years ago. After his death, I interviewed other individuals who knew Jim. They provided additional information on his life. Interviewees included: Corry Kamstra, Debbie Kamstra, Harry J. Kamstra, Jimmy D.H. Kamstra, Sid Kamstra, Ted Kamstra, Andy Koziar, Lynda Supryka (nee Rundle), David Peterson, Alex Pol, Ria Stolk, Paul Ten Westeneind, and Morley Travis.

This book attempts to be an accurate portrayal of Jim based on the information that I have gathered, along with my biased memories. I have generally not disguised the names of anyone mentioned except where indicated. I accept responsibility and apologize to anyone that feels they have been misrepresented.

Prologue

Tjebbe Kamstra stared out on to the never-ending swell of the mid Atlantic as he leaned against the railing of the great ship Groote Beer. The ship sailed onward, taking him further and further away from the Netherlands, the land of his birth, the place that he grew up and knew so well. Ahead lay Canada, a vast land of opportunity, or so he had been led to believe. How would he make out in a new land that spoke a different language and had different values? Would he ever be back to his homeland? Would he see his loving mother again?

Tjebbe had never been a man who spent a long time deliberating over various options; however, once he made a decision, he would run with it. He was ready to take a leap of faith and try to make it in Canada, whatever it took. Tjebbe was 23 years old and he had no intention of ever moving back to the land of his ancestors and all the people he knew.

CHAPTER 1

From Where He Came

When one looks into the unfocused eyes of a naked and helpless newborn baby, there is no way of knowing what type of person that baby will become. What personality will he have? What will his dreams be and what will he accomplish? What disasters will he experience? How will he touch the other lives that he crosses over the course of a lifetime? What opportunities will present themselves, and how will he react to those opportunities? So, it would be for Tjebbe (pronounced "Chebba") Kamstra.

Tjebbe was born in the usual way, on May 3, 1930, in the Netherlands, in Meppel, a small town in the Dutch province of Drenthe. It was the start of the Great Depression and times were tough for all, especially for young families. He was the second of five children. His elder brother, Harmen, was born two-years earlier on March 22, 1928 while his only sister, Johanna, arrived on January 5, 1933. His younger brothers came into the world a little later: Sietse on August 12, 1939, and Douwe on February 28, 1941.

Tjebbe was named after his maternal grandfather, Tjebbe

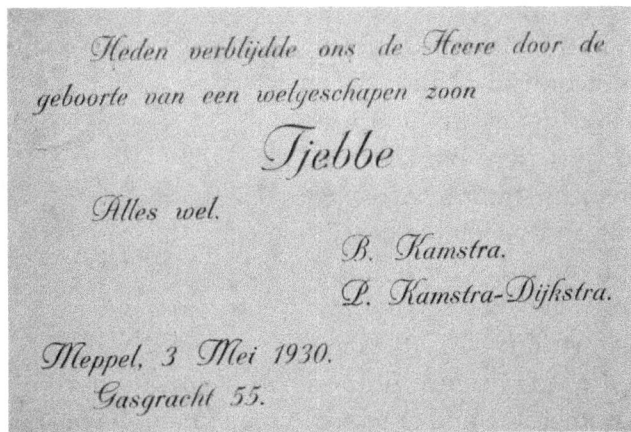

Paper announcing the birth of Tjebbe that was sent to friends and relatives.
Translation: To-day the Lord made us glad with the birth of a well formed son Tjebbe. All is well.

Dykstra, who was married to his grandmother Sietska. It was a Dutch tradition at the time to name the first son after the paternal grandfather and the second son after the maternal grandfather. As a result, in large families, it was common to have several cousins with the same name. Imagine the confusion when relatives got together. Likewise, his brother Harmen, being the oldest, was named after his paternal grandfather. Tjebbe Dykstra died of pneumonia in the 1920s so Tjebbe never met his namesake. Sietska remarried Johannes DeBoer and thus became Sietska DeBoer. His paternal grandfather Harmen, married to Johanna Kamstra, also died of pneumonia in the 1920s. Tjebbe never met that grandfather either.

In the summer of 1927, his parents, Bauke and Pietje, were united in matrimony. Both were 25 years of age. Bauke grew up in town of Makkum, in the province of Friesland, where there was a long line of Kamstras. His bride, Pietje Dykstra, came from the nearby village of Straat. The two of them met while skating on the Friesian canals. Skating was a popular winter activity, for the Dutch, both young and old. With canals spread out across the landscape, skating was a social pastime whenever the winter weather was cold enough.

Although their wedding took place in Makkum, they did not stay there long. The young couple first moved to the coastal town of Harlingen, about 15 km to the north, where Bauke found employment as the manager of a small fruit and vegetable company. They lived there for less than two years when Bauke saw another opportunity. In 1929, he purchased a one-hectare property in Meppel, 90 kilometres away, from his hometown and the people they knew. It was rare for people to move far from the place of their birth.

Tjebbe's parents Pietje and Bauke Kamstra prior to their marriage.

Pietje came from a strong farming background with a strong

will and expectations of her own. She probably had a lot of influence in convincing Bauke to buy that plot of land in another town. Harlingen already had a surplus of market gardeners selling their wares so it would be hard to make a good living there. Meppel, on the other hand, had two rivers, a vibrant Jewish population and a high demand for vegetable produce with less competition. Newcomers were looked upon with suspicion however. As outsiders, it would take many years to be fully accepted by the Meppel townspeople.

But as Pietje had a flair with the customers, they made a place for themselves. She was organized, friendly, and liked interacting with the townspeople. Bauke loved getting his hands dirty, tending to his plants and watching how they bore fruit. He did not particularly like the selling part, but he did need to make money to survive so he rented a small nearby shop where they sold them. He grew strawberries, plums, pears, melons, cucumbers, cabbage, potatoes, carrots and more. His little garden proliferated. He built a small greenhouse so his plants could be propagated early in spring..

In addition to the crops grown in their own garden, they purchased wholesale produce and other food items to sell in the shop. They also bought and sold herring which they pickled in a barrel with vinegar. They made *rollmups*, pickled herrings in a roll, and they made sauerkraut, by stuffing a wooden barrel with shredded cabbage and salt, then letting it ferment with a large stone weighing down the lid. These were the depression years where work and money were scarce so they did whatever they could to support the family. The business was quite successful; they even sold some of the vegetables that they grew to wholesalers who would export it to Germany.

Bauke had a large a tricycle cart known as a *hondenkar* (dog cart) that he pedalled to sell vegetables door to door. As young children, Tjebbe and Harmen, and sometimes Johanna had to help with the neighbourhood rounds. In the late 1930s, Harmen and Tjebbe spent many hours of many days pulling or pushing this cart up and down cobblestone streets. Sometimes other children would see them, and taunt them, yelling "*drek hond*" (push dog), then run away laughing.

Why is father so hard? Tjebbe thought on many occasions. *Why can't he be more like his brother, Jorke, who is such a kind father to my cousins?*

Bauke was strict, no time for play as far as he was concerned, and it did not take much to set off his temper. He would beat the boys if they did not do what he said. He expected obedience and hard work from his children and tolerated no backtalk. Punishing children with beatings was how most parents applied discipline, so their father was not unique in that respect. However, he did seem harsh and beatings were sometimes severe. Tjebbe felt that he had been deprived part of his childhood because so much of it was spent working for his father.

Tjebbe hated the hondenkar and having to work nearly all the

Harmen at age 8, Tjebbe at age 6. *Tjebbe at age 9.*

time. Many times, they had to push those wobbly wheels on cobbled streets through pouring rain with frigid fingers. His schoolmates would be off playing games yet he and his brother had to struggle with the heavy-laden wagon and his heavy-handed father. One positive outcome of this misery is it forged a close bond between the brothers.

Later Bauke acquired a larger wagon pulled by a horse to cart fruits and vegetables to customers. At least now the horse was doing the pulling, but it meant they could take more goods and therefore stay out longer. Bauke would knock on a door, and then make small talk while trying to sell. Bauke could talk and talk, and the Bible was his favourite topic. If he could steer the conversation in that direction, then there was no telling how long it would last. Sometimes he would be invited inside. Bauke seemed to forget why he was there, ending up in a long discussion with the would-be customer. Meanwhile, Tjebbe and Harmen stood out in the street waiting as time ticked by. They would often get home late and have sold less than they had set out to. Upon their return home, Pietje was unimpressed but sympathetic to the boys. She said little to Bauke for she knew how he would react.

In addition to the door-to-door sales, Harmen and Tjebbe

spent much time working the family garden: planting, watering, weeding, and harvesting. Whatever had to be done, they did it. They had no choice. On the bright side, Bauke allowed Tjebbe to have his very own little garden plot, planting a seed for his life-long love for growing plants.

No doubt, Bauke was an authoritarian father figure. He believed that his children should pull their weight and contribute to the family household, and not waste their time in idle play, such as sports, or other ungodly pastimes. He was the eldest of seven children, born into a strict religious family on February 22, 1902. Children then knew that they were to obey their parents without question, or suffer the consequences, which meant a beating. Bauke's own father, Harmen, died of pneumonia in 1929, when Bauke was only 18. Being the eldest, the responsibility of supporting the family and raising his siblings was thrust upon him. He had no choice but to work long hours for six days a week then hand over his meagre wages to his mother. Those tough times likely played a big role in forming Bauke's unyielding character and his harsh parenting of Tjebbe and his siblings.

Bauke was devout, characterized by an unshakable faith. He was a member of the Dutch Christian Reformed Church, while Pietje belonged to the more liberal Protestant Reformed Church. Bauke may have felt that he should have married someone from the same church since religion was so important to him and their differing views created stress in their relationship. Neverthless, both left their respective churches to join the Pentecostal sect. Perhaps this was some kind of attempt to develop a closer bond, but they never did become spiritually unified. Nevertheless, Bauke and Pietje attended church every Sunday with their children in tow. Tjebbe dreaded these two hour-long services. His mind wandered through the long-winded "fire and brimstone" services that wasted much of his precious Sundays, the only day he did not have to work.

Bauke and Pietje argued frequently, and over many things besides religion. The children usually sided with their mother in these arguments which infuriated Bauke even more. Bauke's religious fervour had other effects on the children. Harmen, Tjebbe, and Johanna were not allowed to attend birthday parties or other celebrations with people who he considered to be non-believers. They were not allowed to play soccer or play musical instruments or watch parades. Why? Because these pastimes did not lead to God.

Pietje was a contrast. While also a strong believer, she was a loving mother, protective of her children, and was willing to give them a greater level of freedom. Bauke was the man and head of the household, Pietje could only do so much to soften her husband's wrath. In another time that marriage may not have persisted. Then, however, couples stayed together no matter how caustic their situation became.

Bauke had tried several entrepreneurial ventures but they did not always work out well. Once he purchased a thousand ducklings with the intent of raising them to adulthood, then selling them for meat. He constructed a fenced pen in the backyard where they were kept and fed. Unfortunately, a disease swept through the colony causing many to die and others became so emaciated that they had to be euthanized. In the end few could be sold.

Sometimes, thinking it was a good price, he bought more produce than he could possibly sell, then much of it rotted and had to be discarded. Wholesalers would come to the house to collect their money. Bauke had accrued bad debts on more than one occasion from bad business deals. Sometimes the only way he could pay was by borrowing money from Pietje's brother, Rinze. Despite Bauke`s own inefficiencies, he demanded much from his sons. Tjebbe learned a lot about business from his father, but mostly he learned what *not* to do.

But Tjebbe did share one passion with his father. During the spring of the year, Bauke would wander through the open meadows near Meppel engaged in his favourite activity, *eieren zoeken* (egg hunting). He would listen for the familiar calls then search for the vocalist. When he encountered a bird that appeared to be near a nest, he would freeze then intently observe the bird's activity. If he was lucky the bird would slink back to its nest, leading him to the treasured eggs. If the eggs were fresh, he would collect them for the breakfast table. He pursued the larger birds, particularly the ground-nesting shorebirds. Bauke would look for the *grotto* (Black-tailed Godwit), *wulp* (Eurasian Curlew), *scholekster* (Oystercatcher), and *einden* (ducks). His favourite though was the *kievet* (Lapwing) with its distinctive long-plumed head and piercing cry. *Eieren zoeken* has a long tradition in the northern Netherlands that continues to this day.

Eggs found before the middle of April could be legally harvested since they could be destroyed by frost, and it was early in the nesting season so birds would lay replacements. There was also a tradition that the first kievet egg found in the spring of any year would be presented to the Queen of Holland and the finder would receive 25 guilders, a hefty sum in those days. One spring (probably 1946) Bauke found this special egg and received the reward. The prestige was more valued than the money. Tjebbe was proud of his father for such nationally noteworthy recognition.

Tjebbe and Harmen often went *eieren zoeken* with Bauke. Tjebbe treasured these spring morning rendezvous. These were some of the best times with his father. Nothing beat being out in the pastoral landscape at this time of year when bird song filled the air. The challenge of the hunt added a level of excitement to the quest, testing man against wild animal. When a bird flushed from the ground, they had to fixate on that spot, then scan diligently to pick out the barely discernible mottled eggs, so perfectly camouflaged. The eggs were collected for a small feast later. The delicate taste of a *kievet* egg was superior to any from a domestic chicken or duck.

Bauke had a fondness for the birds themselves, not just their eggs. At one point (probably 1938) he took an old wagon wheel, hoisted it up about ten metres to a broken treetop in the backyard, and fastened it horizontally. Next, he placed a mound of medium-sized sticks on top of the wheel. The following spring a pair of White Storks flew in to claim that tangle of sticks. The birds rearranged the branches into a workable nest and proceeded to lay their eggs there. Bauke was thrilled: success! It became his pride and joy. He watched the courtship and all of the life stages, from incubation, carrying in food, feeding the young, and finally fledging. The birds returned each spring to raise successive families for several years. Having a nest in one's yard was an honour, for there were only a few within the town of Meppel.

Apart from the *eieren zoeken* to eat, Tjebbe also stole eggs out of bird nests to amass a great collection with the goal of acquiring one example from as many different species as he could find. He would pierce a small hole at either end of the egg, then blow out forcibly through the top until all of the yolk and albumen were expelled out the other end. The egg was then a hollow shell and perfectly preserved, but of course, it was delicate. The eggs were carefully placed in firm cigar boxes. He had collected eggs from about forty different species. His most prized was a Mute Swan egg, for not only was it the largest, but the riskiest to obtain. To get it, Tjebbe approached the nest and then was attacked by a furious flapping and hissing male which was big and strong enough to cause serious harm. He used an oar to ward off the great white bird, so he could steal just one of the eggs.

Bauke had taught Tjebbe to keep an ever-watchful eye on the feathered animals in the spring to see if it might betray the location of their nest. Tjebbe scanned treetops and thickets for clumps of sticks that could be a nest complete with a clutch. When a nest was spotted precariously in a treetop, the thrill of the hunt was on. No nest was safe once Tjebbe had spotted it. Many a time he was up a tree, swaying in the upper branches, reaching out for one type of nest or another. One of his prized finds occurred when he dared to climb to the top of a conifer to get at a falcon's nest. Those reddish blotched eggs were a real prize in his collection. He needed to use both hands to climb back down, so he carefully placed a couple of eggs in his mouth. He and the eggs made it down safely.

If the nest contained young birds, sometimes Tjebbe would take them home to raise as pets. If the birds were just hatchlings he would return in a week when they were bigger before robbing the nest. Many a young bird were thus raised. He would put them in a makeshift cage, then forage for worms and insects to feed them. The magpies were his favourite, with their beautiful black and white pattern and long streaming tail. They were also intelligent, noisy, and mischievous. He raised crows, jackdaws, and Wood Pigeons. As tame as they were, the birds were free-flying and would usually leave on their own by summer's end.

When their younger brother, Sietse, was born in the summer of 1939, Tjebbe was sent away. He stayed with his grandmother, Sietska de Boer, in Schraat, Friesland for about a month. This was to make things easier for Pietje as she would have to tend to the needs of the newborn. It was a happy time for the nine-year-old Tjebbe. He accompanied his grandfather delivering mail around the town while grandmother spoiled him. He played with cousins that he rarely saw, and he fished in the canal. It was a relief to be away from his father for a while.

When Tjebbe returned home, however, he regretted ever going away. His best friend was a lively little dog that he named "Tomi". Tomi could root out rats and other rodents with great fury. The little mutt loved Tjebbe right back and would follow him everywhere – the two were inseparable.

The dog could not come to the grandparents, so it had to stay in Meppel in the care of Bauke. The poor dog was obsessively loyal to Tjebbe and no one else. Missing its master so much, the dog refused to eat or drink; he moped about and hardly moved. Without Tjebbe it lost its will to live so died within a week or so. Tjebbe returned to the worst possible homecoming. He was shattered.

CHAPTER 2

World War II and German Occupation

As the 1930s drew to a close, the Dutch economy was finally starting to improve. Bauke was able to afford the purchase of his own store in 1938. However, a sense of unease was spreading across the Netherlands, for things were brewing in their great neighbour on the eastern border. Adolf Hitler was Supreme Chancellor of Germany and he had great aspirations of expanding that nation across Europe.
Germany invaded Poland in September 1939 igniting World War II. The Netherlands declared itself a neutral country in an attempt to stay out of the war, but would this truce be respected by the Germans? Clearly, it was not.

On May 10, 1940 the first of long lines of disciplined German soldiers marched into Meppel, which was only forty kilometres west of the German border. It was an exceptional spectacle to have hundreds of soldiers in uniform, lifting their legs in unison, and even singing as they invaded the town. Their steel soles clattered as the helmeted marchers passed along the streets. Other soldiers paraded in on horse-

German soldiers marching into Meppel in 1940. The boy on the right is Harmen.

back. Spoke-wheeled artillery and wagons were hauled in by horses. There were hundreds of them. The sight of so many invaders and the cacophony struck terror into the onlooking civilians.

The Kamstra family stood on the street staring at the procession. Pietje was crying, she knew this meant that the Netherlands was now an occupied country placed under German rule. Soldiers went door-to-door, entering houses to check the premises for potential snipers. An officer stopped in front of Bauke, pointed to the open upstairs window. "Go up and shut that window immediately," he barked. Bauke ran upstairs to do just that.

Tjebbe was not afraid, but he did not appreciate the enormity of the moment. To a boy of ten, the sight of so many triumphant marchers and the volume of moving machinery was nothing short of spectacular. He did not feel the anxiety of responsibility that his parents and all adults would have. The Dutch army was insignificant with outdated equipment compared to the mighty German war machine that advanced from the east. Nevertheless, the proud Dutch were not about to be taken over without a fight. Before the Germans arrived in Meppel, Harmen was briefly hired to guide Dutch soldiers that were not familiar with this part of the country. The Dutch resistance at Rotterdam, in the south part of the country, caused significant casualties to the Germans in the first days of the invasion. But after that city was bombed, the Dutch government surrendered, only five days into the war.

Some of Tjebbe's relatives were soldiers in that battle. Pietje's brother, Tjebbe Dykstra, was captured, taken prisoner and sent to Germany. To everyone's relief, he was released and returned home about a month later. Nevertheless, the entire country would be under complete German control for almost five years.

Germans were viewed as a relatively benign enemy at the beginning of the war. There were close historic ties between the two countries, and many had relatives on either side of the border. Thus, the German administration was not as harsh or constraining on the Dutch populace as they were in the other countries that they invaded. Adolf Hitler considered the Dutch to be part of the Aryan race, the tall blonde-haired, blue-eyed Germanic type people, that he considered to be superior.

It was not the same for the Jewish population in the Netherlands, however. Meppel contained a sizeable Jewish population at the beginning of the war and multitudes had their properties confiscated. The Dutch police were tasked with rounding them up and forcing them onto trains that carted them off to one of several concentration camps set up in the Netherlands. The Kamstra family knew many Jewish people as customers and Tjebbe had several Jewish friends in town who disappeared in this period. He never saw any of them again.

The Germans enforced a policy of *Gleichschaltung* ("enforced conformity"), and outlawed all political parties, except for the National Socialist Movement (known as the NSB) which was Nazism. New restrictions were imposed. Curfews mandated that no civilians were allowed out of their homes from 8:00 pm to 6:00 am.

Only once was Tjebbe ever out after curfew, and it was for a legitimate reason. One evening he was playing with a scythe, swinging it back and forth as if it was a harmless toy. His hand slipped off the handle and into the razor-sharp blade. It sliced deep into the skin between his fingers. He screamed, blood spurting out and dribbling onto the ground. Pietje wrapped a rag around his hand but couldn't get the bleeding to stop. In desperation, Bauke called the police. A German soldier soon arrived at the door who immediately carted the boy off to the doctor for stitching.

Bauke however, broke curfew on several occasions, going out to the barber for a shave or to visit a friend. A bit a risky for a trivial reason perhaps, however, there were no streetlights on in town, so he felt secure venturing out. Fortunately, he never got caught.

An underground civilian resistance known as *Onderdyker* soon formed in Meppel as it did in many towns across the country. They would send messages to the Allied forces about German intelligence, hide persecuted people, and generally mess up German military maneuvers wherever possible. Tjebbe's family was not involved but when the war was over, they learned that some friends and neighbours had been active clandestine participants. Pietje was conflicted. She felt that it was a duty to her country to help the resistance if they could. Bauke forbade it however, he was afraid for himself and the possible repercussions for his family. Besides as far as he was concerned, the German presence wasn't so bad.

Even in war people need to eat, work, raise their children and life must carry on. Bauke kept growing and selling produce as before. Food production was an essential endeavour consequently the Kamstra family never suffered serious shortages that many of their fellow countrymen experienced. They also were able to exchange vegetables for milk and meat with local farmers. Pietje would skim off the cream and churn the fat-rich milk into butter.

Pietje and Bauke standing in front of their store in Meppel. This photo was taken after the war in 1954.

Life attained some level of normalcy despite the imposed German restrictions and the ever-present foreigners. Tjebbe, Harmen, and Johanna continued to attend classes at school, at least for a while. Then one day teachers notified them that the school would close, and classes would be cancelled as the classrooms were converted into barracks for German soldiers. Education did not cease entirely, however; students went to the homes of their teachers for brief instruction and to pick up their assignments. Homework was completed independently (or with the help of their parents) and returned to the teacher for marking. Not the best learning environment for sure, but the community felt education was too important to abandon entirely and this solution was the best they could do.

Tjebbe and Harmen would have to drag the wagon loaded with precious greens to army barracks that had been their school. Bauke had no choice but to sell potatoes and vegetables to the army, but at least he was paid for it. Harmen, being a teenager, was recruited along with other Dutch youths to work at nearby German fortifications, digging trenches and performing other menial tasks. These youngsters did not put a lot of effort into the tasks they were assigned, however, and the supervising soldiers were quite lenient to their slave labour.

Bauke also ended up working for the Germans. A German officer, who was stationed nearby, occasionally dropped by the store, instructing Bauke to mail his letters to Germany. Since Bauke was fluent in German, the officer could converse with him and the two became friendly. Due to this relationship, Bauke was able to travel to Germany. For eighteen months, between 1942 to 1943, he worked on a farm growing vegetables there. He only returned home once or twice during this period. Many Dutchmen went to Nazi Germany for employment during this period since work had become so scarce in the Netherlands. Bauke's brothers Jorke and Douwe also went. Nevertheless, those that left for Germany were viewed as sympathizers, working to help the enemy. Tjebbe felt ashamed of his father on this account.

In Bauke's absence, Pietje could run the store without interference. She made sure that the shelves were properly stocked (given the wartime limitations), customers were looked after, and bills were paid on time. However, the back garden was not being tended to as it had been destroyed by the soldiers who trampled it to in order to erect a tank wall there. Pietje sourced produce from elsewhere and sold it instead. Tjebbe and Harmen carted the produce to customers around the town, but now without their father and the dreaded *hondenkar*.

When Bauke returned home and resumed charge of the family business, he found a new location to replant the vegetable garden. Before long he was able to sell his own harvest. Good thing, too. Produce was getting harder and harder to obtain from outside sources, and surprisingly, few people in the town grew their own vegetables. The garden's bounty could be bartered with nearby farmers for meat or milk, and with other shopkeepers in exchange for other foods and goods.

Bartering had become a way of life. Having vegetables and other produce to trade was better than cash. Bauke even grew some low-grade tobacco. It may have been poor quality snuff, but any tobacco was highly valued in the bartering economy. The family also raised rabbits for sale as well as for their own consumption. Tjebbe was tasked with raising the gentle, long-eared animals. Each day he gathered arms full of long grass for forage and cleaned the poop out their pens. He also had the less pleasant tasks of killing, skinning, and gutting the same animals that he had grown fond of.

Scarcity breeds resourcefulness and Tjebbe was gifted at making do with what was available. When bicycle tires wore out beyond repair, he attached a section of stiff rubber garden hose to the rims. It made for a hard ride, where the rider was jolted with every bump in the road. Also, each wheel rotation ended with a "thump" where the end of the hose connected to itself. It was apparent that Tjebbe had a gift for finding mechanical solutions to many problems. `

Maintaining health and hygiene under wartime conditions proved to be a challenge, however. Tjebbe developed a sore throat, fever and red skin rash characteristic of Scarlet Fever. These symptoms soon passed on to Harmen, Sietse and Douwe, but Johanna, strong girl that she was, never contracted it. The authorities placed the house under quarantine for six weeks as a means of preventing its spread to other people. The children could never leave the house over this period and when it was over, all of the clothes that they had worn had to be burned. New clothes were not available for purchase, so they used whatever hand-me-downs they could find.

The Netherlands, situated midway between England and Germany, lay directly on the flight path of German planes on bombing raids across the English Channel, or for eastward British bombers attempting to cripple German cities and industries. Tjebbe looked up to the sky with delight whenever the great noisy birds soared overhead. Rarely were bombs dropped on this land, so the planes were generally not viewed as a threat as they would be in the destination countries.

Tjebbe acquired a small book that identified the silhouettes of the various types of planes from both sides. It was like a bird field guide. There were dozens of types: fighters, bombers, and flying boxcars; German Messerschmitts and Focke-Wulfs, and British Grumman Hellcats, Lancasters, and Spitfires. Tjebbe studied the book and soon became an expert, able to recognize almost any plane that roared overhead, first by its shape and eventually by the pitch of the engine roar. This was the start of a lifelong love of airplanes.

One day in the summer of 1944, a distressed American B17 four-engine bomber dropped some shells on Meppel then made an emergency crash landing in a shallow lake about five km west of town. A section of town was destroyed, and a handful of townspeople were killed. When he heard about the downed plane, Tjebbe thought it was an opportunity too good to pass up: two of his school mates, Tamo Hazelaar and Walter Buter, were also up for an adventure. The three boys rowed out from Meppel in Tamo's narrow rowboat in the direction of the fallen bomber. Taking turns on the oars, it took the boys hours to negotiate the ten km distance through canals.

Once on the lake, they caught sight of the majestic-winged structure sitting silently in the tranquil waters. They approached cautiously then climbed into the hull of the half-submerged craft. Tjebbe climbed into the cockpit to examine the complex instrumentation. Then he explored the passageway, looking for any items that could be useful. They entered machine gun turrets on top and in the plane's nose, pretending they were firing away at enemy aircraft. A distant buzz was first ignored but as it grew louder, the boys realized that aircraft were heading in their direction. Tjebbe stuck his out of a hatch to see. They were American!

All three scrambled out of the turret and into the rowboat, rowing the awkward boat as fast as it could go, terrified that the planes would unleash gunfire at any second. None came but the young adventurers kept pulling water, eager to return home in one piece. They did not try that again, but that wasn't the only near-miss for Tjebbe, who as a curious 11-year-old boy, could not resist exploring the debris of war.

Sometimes Tjebbe and his friends would look for and find unexploded ammunition. Using simple tools, they would dismantle live shells, and take out the gunpowder to make fireworks, or just light a match and watch it burn. They would learn the hard way that these were not playthings. Tjebbe heard about another American warplane that had crashed in the fields on the outskirts of town.

"There's sure to be some ammo and other neat stuff in there!" he heard a boy say.

Without hesitation, Tjebbe and his buddy Alex Wieting went on a salvage mission. They ventured out to the unguarded site when no adults were looking. They poked around the twisted fuselage of the plane wreck, to see what they could find. Tjebbe pulled out wires, extracted flight instruments and found a number of unspent cartridges. Success, they brought home a good load of booty without their parents knowing. It was the gunpowder that they wanted most, which would have to somehow get extracted from the casings. Alex had the wise idea of strapping one of the larger shells into a vice. Then he hit the igniter end of the bullet with a hammer thinking the bullet would shoot out forward. A sudden explosion, with a flash of light and the end of one of Alex's finger was blown off. He was lucky that was all he lost.

Tjebbe witnessed some real war action on a few occasions. While visiting Staphorst, a village not far south of Meppel, he heard roaring engines overhead. He looked up to see a fleet of allied aircraft. They circled overhead, then a couple of planes descended into a dive, opening machine gunfire onto a nearby train containing supplies and wounded German soldiers. Bullets ricocheted off boxcars and soldiers dropped to the ground in the ensuing battle. Tjebbe and villagers took cover.

On another occasion, behind the family home, he saw German machine-gunners positioned on their perches on railway cars engaged in a shoot-out. "Rat-tat-tat". Allied fighter planes descended from the sky, spraying a cacophony of bullets on their adversaries. Then they lurched back upwards to disappear from view. Tjebbe was quickly called back inside to take cover.

Then on Harmen's 14th birthday, March 22, 1942, a German ammunition train stationed in Meppel caught fire. Whether it was arson or an accident, the cause was not known. Tjebbe, his family and neighbours gawked at the spectacle from a safe distance as fifteen boxcars were enshrouded in flame and smoke. Then they heard a great blast as the sides blew out of one boxcar followed by one explosion after another punctuated the crackling inferno. A dangerous show of unintended fireworks, with great blasts, pops, and bangs filled the night sky.

Several days later when the fire had fizzled out, Tjebbe and his friend Albert Vaartjes, investigated the blackened ruins. Contorted metal and splintered wood were scattered everywhere. An unexploded shell about 40 centimetres long with a pointed warhead lay on the ground. Albert walked over and picked up the heavy cylindrical object, examined it carefully, then threw it as far as he could. It clattered to the ground and exploded with a terrible blast, ripping off most of Albert's leg.

Albert screeched in agony. Tjebbe was dumbstruck by the horror of spattered blood, exposed bone, and the severed limb. Not knowing what else to do he ran as fast as he could to get help. Adults soon arrived to carry the wounded boy home and another adult hurried off to get the doctor. The doctor arrived but his face showed that the chance of recovery was slim. He did his best to bandage up the catastrophic wound. Days later Albert died.

As the war dragged on, food and other goods became even scarcer. Ration cards were issued to the populace and these were essential for obtaining food. The winter of 1944-45 was particularly severe and cold, testing the metal of the Dutch people. The German supply line was breaking down and most of the available food was diverted to the soldiers, not the civilians. The densely populated western part of Holland was in a particularly dire situation. They were out of food, people were starving, and many were dying. People had resorted to eating tulip bulbs or anything that might provide some nutrition but even that did not sustain them for long. For any chance of surviving, people had to get out. They did by train or on foot, flooding into the eastern areas, including near Meppel, where shortages were not quite as severe.

One day a German supply train was moving along on the outskirts of Meppel when the US Air Force descended upon it with a barrage of firepower. P51 Mustangs swooped in machine-gunning the boxcars while the locomotive was torpedoed. The Germans were not prepared, many soldiers were killed, another train was destroyed, and any survivors fled. The army abandoned fully stocked cars containing boxes of uniforms, weaponry, packaged food, and other supplies.

The town's people did not wait. They scrambled out to the train to scavenge whatever they could, given the general scarcity of nearly everything by this point. Tjebbe was eager to claim some of this booty too but his father forbade him from doing so. Bauke felt it was not a Christian thing to do. Despite everything that the Germans had done to the Dutch, salvaging stuff from the train was still stealing and therefore a sin. Tjebbe could not understand or agree with this thinking but he did not disobey.

Firewood was also in short supply. Early in the war town folk salvaged railway ties for this purpose. Germans had pulled up the steel rails so that the metal could be melted down and refabricated into weaponry as part of their 'war machine'. The squared and creosote covered wooded ties were left. Tjebbe was sent out to gather ties. He sawed the blackened timbers into a workable size, then hauled them home to be burned in the stove for heating and cooking. The aroma of burning creosote may have been unpleasant but at least the house was warm. By 1944, the ties and any other old loose lumber had long been scavenged. Finding more wood became increasingly difficult.

Tjebbe and his friend Klaas Slomp were told by their parents, to find some much-needed fuelwood. Out with an axe, they came across a suitable specimen tree for their needs, so they chopped it down. They knew that the tree stood on the property of a wealthy farmer, and there he was heading in their direction. The boys grabbed the ax and bolted before they could be recognized.

The angry farmer yelled out then took chase after them. Propelled by fear the youths were faster. They ran along the railway, then down the embankment into a tall reed bed. Panting heavily Tjebbe and Klaas pulled down clumps of the long-dried stalks, covering themselves, then they lay as still as they could. The farmer soon came stomp stomping along the railway, right past where the boys were hiding. He had been outsmarted.

The boys crawled out from under the reed and made it home unscathed but without any firewood. With no fuel, Pietje could not cook. They would have to find wood somewhere else another day. How much longer would they have to live like this?

CHAPTER 3

Coming of Age in Peacetime

At the start of 1945, it was apparent that the tide was beginning to turn for the unwelcome invaders. They were losing their stronghold. One day in early April Tjebbe saw two German soldiers marching along the street pointing their guns at two English-speaking soldiers that had been captured. These were the first Canadians that he had ever seen. But soon they would be seeing many more, for the Canadian infantry played a major role in the liberation of the Netherlands. Starting at the Belgian border Canadians fought their way northward as the Germans were in retreat. Canadian tanks, jeeps, trucks, and other artillery arrived in Meppel in April. By this point the Germans were no longer putting up much resistance but were falling back, perhaps sensing that defeat was imminent. The German militia blew up many of the bridges once they had crossed to slow down the advancing liberators.

Germany officially surrendered on May 4, 1945. Finally, the Netherlands was free of its stranglehold. Men and women of all ages poured into the streets to rejoice. Canadian tanks slowly ground their way into town with soldiers protruding from open hatches. Young Dutch women rode on top with their liberators. There was a sense of jubilation and optimism in town and across the nation. They had survived and the war was over.

People were dancing in the streets, cheering, greeting each other. The liberating soldiers came with goodies that were distributed to the townsfolk. Items that hadn't been available in years suddenly appeared in abundance. Candies, cigarettes, biscuits, white bread, canned meat, dates, clothing. Once distribution lines were re-established, Uncle Peter Dykstra, Pietje's brother who lived in California, shipped them boxes of clothing and other luxuries.

During the war, some of the town's people worked closely with the German army, assisting them to their own benefit. Those

People celebrating in the streets of Meppel at the end of WWII in May 1945. Sietse is the small boy at far left. Tjebbe is the blonde boy in the centre.

who collaborated with the enemy were rounded up at gunpoint then lined up in the centre of the street for a public shaming. Sietse and Tjebbe looked on and knew some of these people. With guns pointed and harsh words from the crowd, the boys were terrified that the traitors were going to be executed in front of their eyes. They were not, however, and the crowd eventually dissipated.

Over several months, the country began to rebuild itself. People saw gradual improvements in the economy and living conditions. Tjebbe was now an adolescent of 15 years. Schools re-opened, but instead of returning to his public school, Tjebbe attended Ambacht, a trade school in Meppel. He had regular classes by day, and at night he learned about motor mechanics. The workings of engines fascinated the young lad. He had a natural ability for figuring out how they worked and as he tinkered, he was also learning how to fix them.

Before long he found work in an auto garage as a mechanics assistant for Piet Jagersma. Tjebbe enjoyed the work; he was learning on the job and taking home 10 guilders per week. His father, however, felt that the boss was taking advantage of him, and told him that he should demand more. The next day Tjebbe reluctantly approached Piet to ask for an increase in his wage. Piet said that he could not afford to pay any more, so instead he laid him off. Now out of work, Bauke asked him to help out in the family vegetable business. Tjebbe worked there for a short while but it was the last thing he wanted to do.

Meanwhile, brother Harmen turned eighteen in 1946 and so was conscripted into the rejuvenated Dutch army. His call of duty would take him to Indonesia. Indonesia had been a Dutch colony for several hundred years prior to World War II. Between the German occupation of the homeland and the Japanese occupation of Indonesia, the Netherlands had lost most of its control of the colony. The restored Dutch government wanted it back and were sending in troops to get it. But Indonesians would no longer put up with their colonial status. The country was on the cusp of civil war, and therefore this was a potentially dangerous posting. Harmen feared that he may not return alive.

Harmen was given a furlough before his tour of duty. The two brothers set out together on a two-week bicycle trip to visit various relatives all around the Netherlands, possibly to see them for the last time. They first rode north to Friesland, a stronghold of the Kamstra clan. The lads were welcomed by uncles, aunts, and cousins wherever they went they would be fed and put up for the night. They peddled across the Afsluidijk to North Holland, a 30-kilometre-long dyke that separates the Ijsselmeer (a freshwater lake that was once an arm of the sea) from the North Sea. Some nights when not with relatives they took refuge in whatever barn they could find. They slept in haylofts, making sure that the farmers who owned them did not notice them.

When they made it to Amsterdam, Harmen snuck Tjebbe into the army barracks where he was stationed, to stay overnight. This was fine by his fellow privates, but when a commanding officer found Tjebbe there, he was not pleased. He turfed out Tjebbe and reprimanded Harmen since barracks were off-limits to civilians.

Pedalling further along, away from the big city, they encountered two attractive young ladies stopped along the roadside with their bicycles. One had a flat tire, and she wasn't sure what to do. This was a simple task for handy lads. They repaired the tire, impressing the girls. Harmen had a way with words especially when there were members of the opposite sex to charm. He was funny and clever, giving the girls subtle compliments, making one blush. Tjebbe felt awkward compared to his smooth-talking brother, who was more forthright. Harmen invited the girls over for a visit to Meppel. They were enchanted so followed along on their bikes to the Kamstra home. They were all welcomed by Pietje who knew one of the girl's families. What a coincidence, she was from the same hometown. Not long thereafter, Harmen was sent to Indonesia, where he would be stationed for two years.

While their older brother was away, Tjebbe did not neglect his younger brother, Sietse. At age 15, Tjebbe rode his bicycle from Meppel to Makkum, a distance of approximately 100 kilometres, with six-year-old Sietse sitting on the rack over the rear wheel, clinging onto his back. The uncomfortable ride took the entire day, but at least there were no hills to contend with. The cute boy and his talkative big brother were welcomed by their Uncle Jorke and other relatives who teased them about their sore butts. The boys rode back home the next day.

Tjebbe with Sietse on the back of the bicycle.

In little Sietse's eyes, Tjebbe was so big, strong, and wise in the ways of the world. Tjebbe taught him how to carve a whistle. He found a perfectly straight section of a willow twig, tapped the soft bark with a knife handle for several minutes. The bark would slide off the hardwood core in one piece. He would carve grooves and slots in the wood, slide the bark back on, and presto: it made a loud high-pitched whistle when one blew through it. Tjebbe made a wicked slingshot from a car tire tube strapped on a forked branch.

Tjebbe also had a real skill for fashioning a kite from simple materials and he could fly it skillfully. Sometimes twenty neighbourhood boys would be standing in a field on a breezy day, each with their hand on a string attached to their own flying creations. Sietse marvelled how his brother's kite sailed through the air better than any of the others. That is my brother, thought Sietse. He was so proud.

They also wandered fields in spring eieren zoeken, egg hunting. Tjebbe had learned the secrets of nest finding from Bauke and now he was passing on that knowledge. "Watch carefully for the spot where the bird first flushes" he instructed. "That is where the nest is going to be".

He taught Sietse how to fish the canals with a bamboo pole, a string, and a floating bobber. One time the two were holding their pole with lines in the water at a favourite spot. The local fishmonger rode by on his bicycle, stopping near the boys. The old man had a bucketful of entrails from fish that he had gutted. He maliciously tossed the bucket's contents onto Sietse's line and floating bobber. The boy was very upset seeing the slimy mess of intestines, scales, and fins tangled in his fishing gear. The brothers cleaned off the slop, cursing the miserable lout under their breaths. Then they saw ripples on the water surface—other fish were coming to feast on the guts. A revelation came to the boys. This was such a good fishing spot because the fishmonger regularly dumped his waste here.

Tjebbe was growing into a capable, determined and self-reliant young man. He had grown to a full 180 centimetres in height, nearly six feet, and had a muscular build without an ounce of fat. With his wavy blonde locks and strong aquiline nose, he felt ready to set forth in the world. He applied for work on a freighter ship and was offered the job. The only catch was that he needed his father's permission as he was only 16. Tjebbe approached the subject delicately fearing that his father would find some reason that he should not go to sea. To his surprise, Bauke was impressed that Tjebbe had taken such initiative so he gave him his blessing.

So, in the spring of 1946, Tjebbe set off to Groningen on the north coast where he boarded a great iron vessel that went by the name of Drittura. He felt awed by the massive engines and the sound of pumping pistons that propelled this beast. His first time out of the Netherlands, Tjebbe rode the ship on the North Sea for six months, sailing back and forth between Germany, Norway, Sweden, and

England. He was a helmsman, responsible for a range of tasks from scrubbing floors, painting over the rusting metal, tarring the deck, and when he was lucky, steering the ship. The Drittura was a cargo carrier. On many runs it picked up scrap iron (mostly disused military hardware left over from the war) in Hamburg then transported it to smelters in England.

Hamburg was a dilapidated, sad-looking, shell of a city so soon after the war. It was characterized by partially standing structures, skeletons of factories and pock-marked walls after the heavy allied bombing a few years previous. Things were looking up there too, however, with some new industrial buildings under construction. Ship work was hard but satisfying. The cycle: 12-hour days for four days, then four days off. He was now raking in 150 guilders per month, more pay then he had ever seen. This made him happy.

One day while in one of the ports, Tjebbe ran into an old friend who sailed on another Dutch merchant ship. He was invited on board for a visit and a drink. Tjebbe was introduced to the captain who offered him 200 guilders per month to work that ship, a substantial increase. He accepted the offer, went home for a couple of weeks, then set off on the fine ship working alongside an old mate.

A dashing Tjebbe ready to take on the world in the merchant marine.

Not for long, however, for after only a month, Tjebbe received an even better offer on the deck of the *Europa*, docked in Antwerp. He just had to find a way to Belgium. The *Europa* mainly sailed between Antwerp and London but made occasional voyages to other European ports.

Sailors were an unrefined lot. Although not really Tjebbe's type he soon learned to fit in, and he was fine with being on the water. No slacking on this job which suited him fine. Work was hours-long and arduous but there were opportunities to go ashore in one port or another. He frequented seedy bars in the company of his shipmates.

Sailors had access to a quota of duty-free liquor, cigarettes, and other goods that they could sell. There was always someone willing to buy contraband in any harbour. Developing his entrepreneurial skills, Tjebbe would buy various articles in France then sell them on the black market in England for a healthy profit. During one landing in England, however, a customs officer boarded the ship to search the sailors. They were not stupid; they knew what sailors were up to. Tjebbe was found to have more than his allotted tobacco quota and so was fined £60, a hefty sum (valued at more than ten times that amount today).

Tjebbe and a fellow sailor aboard the good ship Europa.

On one voyage *Europa* was heavily loaded with massive rolls of steel when she plowed out of Liverpool. As they made their way along the west coast of England the sky grew dark, the wind howled, and sea frothed viciously. The ship rode up and down through the rolling swell for what felt like hours, then abruptly struck a sandbar, pitching forward to a halt. Cables snapped, steel rolls broke loose and rolled freely around the deck, crashing into objects, busting crates. Between lodging on the sandbar and the shifted unbalanced weight of the cargo, the long iron vessel buckled and bent in the middle.

Tjebbe was in the bridge when the ship ran aground, and a fellow low-ranking sailor was at the helm, steering. Maritime law dictates that the captain must be on the bridge at all times whenever there are navigation challenges such as inclement weather or hazardous passages. Through that storm, however, the captain was nowhere to be seen. Tjebbe knew where the old son-of-a-gun was — he was below deck drinking liquor.

This was not right, Tjebbe thought. *He had neglected his duty and endangered the whole ship.*

Tjebbe confronted the captain, telling him he was at fault for running aground. The burly captain was not about to stand for such an accusation from a junior sailor. He was furious, cursing madly and threatening to kill him if he brought this case forward or told anyone else. Not sure how unpredictable the captain might be, Tjebbe decided to keep mum. The ship limped on to Zaltbommel in Holland for repairs, 50 kilometres up the Rhine River from Rotterdam. Europa would lie on dry dock for three months while a busy crew made her seaworthy again.

Back on the seas in a freshly painted and repaired version of Europa, Tjebbe sailed a new route, this time south to Safi, Morocco. The ship was equipped with a cable winch to load and unload cargo. A North African port operated on a different culture than the European ones he was used to. It took twice as many workers, twice as long to load and unload the ship's cargo.

Tjebbe scoffed at the poor work ethics of these people. Why were they so lazy? Sugar was one of the main cargo items which was hoisted on the ship in heavy cloth bags. If a sugar bag tore open, the Moroccan sailors and stevedores were allowed to claim the spoils. Every so often a bag would drop on the ground and split open, spilling the sweet white powder onto the deck. Men would scramble scooping up the loose sugar and pulling the bag to the side to claim it. The cloth bags did not break by accident; an exporter could count on losing a small percent of his sugar bags, a cost of doing business in Morocco.

Tjebbe spent eighteen months on the *Europa* before returning to Dutch soil. That was enough sea life for him. In1949, Tjebbe joined the Dutch army as all 18-year-old males were required to do. First, he needed to learn to become a soldier which meant three months of hard military training at an army base in Amersfoort. He learned to fire high powered rifles and machine guns and how to throw live hand grenades without blowing himself up. That was the fun part. Not so fun was the daily physical training and marching.

The military was obsessed with marching. Every six weeks there would be a parade. Hours marching, marching, and more marching. It got tedious. But army life provided other benefits. Tjebbe received a chauffer's training. He learned how to drive with proficiency and how

Tjebbe (centre) in the army with fellow soldiers.

to fix vehicle engines. He loved the hum of a well-tuned engine; it was just like a living thing. A motor sang, increasing in pitch as it accelerated.

Luckily, Indonesia was now independent, so Dutch soldiers were no longer being sent there. Some of the returning soldiers came back with horror stories of bloody encounters. Even Harmen would not talk about what he experienced while he was there. Tjebbe was given another overseas option, however, a tour of duty in Korea (this was at the start of the bloody Korean War). At least he was given a choice, and he did not have to think long before declining this opportunity of high adventure. After a year and a half, his patriotic call of duty completed, Tjebbe returned to civilian life in Meppel.

Meanwhile, brother Harmen who previously had gone through a string of girlfriends finally committed to one. He married his sweetheart Roeli Zanting in 1950. Tjebbe missed the wedding since he was off at military training and could not get away.

Tjebbe's military mechanical training soon paid off in civilian life. In 1951, Tjebbe was hired to help install a boiler and central heating system at a small airport in the town of Havelte, by a company called Atiba. Next Atiba sent him to The Hague to install heating systems. There he met Karin Bowman, a fine-looking lass who took an immediate fancy to him. She worked as a housekeeper for a wealthy baroness.

No average maid, Karin cooked and organized the household and had developed a trusted relationship with the royal dame. Tjebbe saw much of Karin and became romantically involved. One weekend Karin accompanied him to Meppel to meet his parents and family. She made a good impression. Pietje was happy to see her boy with a partner.

Tjebbe signed up for ballroom dance lessons which helped him perfect his dance floor steps. People loved dancing in this town. Every weekend there were dances at one of several big dancehalls in The Hague. Tjebbe was a regular at these events, usually with Karin, but other times on his own. Being able to move gracefully and rhythmically whether two-step or swing, was a ticket to attracting the attention of onlooking young ladies. He never had trouble finding a dance partner.

Tjebbe's old friend Klaas Slomp was in The Hague for a visit. Klaas also had a sharp eye and they both enjoyed the thrill of *eiren zoeken* when they were younger in Meppel, so why not here in The Hague? Tjebbe knew just the place. From a moving train several days earlier, he had spotted a lot of bird activity on the sprawling lands of a large estate on the outskirts of town. That was worth investigating. They arrived early in the morning, hid their bicycles in some bushes then marched off into the open fields in quest of nests. Lapwings were flying about crying "kiewit, kiewit".

"Just keep your eye on the bird and see where it goes," Tjebbe said to Klaas.

One of the tuft-headed birds strutted along the bare ground then sat down. It was a nest, four brown mottled eggs in a slight depression, almost invisible among the soil.

They picked up the eggs, then heard the loud blast of a shotgun from behind. They turned around to see two men walking quickly towards them, one carried a rifle. These must be the *huisbewaarders*, property wardens whose duty it was to protect the estate lands from poachers and trespassers. The friends darted across the open field figuring that they could outrun their older pursuers. This seemed to work, at least until the field ended in a corner at a deep, very wide ditch. They had two choices, either jump in the cold water with their clothes on to swim across or accept capture. They hesitated; the panting wardens were soon upon them.

"You should not be here; this is royal property so you must come with us," one of them stated. "What are your names?"

Tjebbe dutifully told them his. Klaas, however, blurted out the first false name that came into his mind. He did not want to be identified as he was employed as a police officer in another part of Holland. A poaching charge on a royal estate would certainly create complications, possibly marking the end of his career. The young offenders were taken to the police station for further interrogation where Klaas could hide his identity no longer. They were going to be charged for poaching and trespassing.

Tjebbe thought of Karin's royal connection and wondered if she could help in any way. He called her from the police station. Karin explained the situation to her baroness. Unbelievably, the baroness came down to the police station to talk with the constable. The trespass charges were dropped, and no-one was the wiser about Klaas's vocation.

With the Hague work finished, Atiba sent Tjebbe to a job site in the town of Almelo, 200 kilometres to the east, near the German border. Whether it was due to the distance or some other reason, Tjebbe broke up with Karin. She, however, was unwilling to let go; he had stolen her heart.

CHAPTER 4

Leaving the Netherlands

Somewhere Tjebbe developed dissatisfaction with the constraints of his native land. Perhaps it started when he was exposed to other countries with the merchant marine, seeing that things were different in other places. Perhaps it was the crowdedness of this tiny country that appeared so small on the world map that made the opportunities to get ahead so limited. Or maybe it was the fact that so many other Dutch people were pulling up stakes and leaving for distant lands across the ocean. Most were bound for North America or Australia. The idea of starting anew somewhere else really appealed to Tjebbe. One day he made up his mind; he was going to leave too.

His first choice was the United States; now that sounded like the place to be. Maybe his mother's brother, Uncle Peter Dykstra, who had been living in California for years, could sponsor him. Tjebbe wrote a letter. Peter wrote back stating that there was nothing he could do; America had imposed some strict rules for immigration.

Well, so much for the USA, thought Tjebbe.

Then he thought about Canada. Everyone was talking about Canada. The Canadians had liberated his country so they must be really good people. Why, his brother had already emigrated there three years earlier. The Canadian government with its vast sparsely inhabited territory was offering visas for farmers, so that was a possibility. Tjebbe was not a farmer though. But he knew something about growing plants and raising animals due to all that hard work during his childhood, plus the Canadian and Dutch governments even offered a farm training program.

I could become a farmer! It can't be that hard, Tjebbe decided and he signed up for the program, determined to do whatever it took.

He was sent to a farm in a place called Warffum where he worked for almost a year. He learned about growing crops, how to plow with horses (an antiquated method even by that time), and how

Groote Beer, the ship that took Tjebbe and many other Dutch people to Canada.

to operate a tractor. Then he did a stint at a dairy farm in the small village of Amen, in the province of Drenthe for another six months. There he learned about animal husbandry and how to milk the beasts both by hand and machine.

Tjebbe was not paid for these agricultural adventures save for room and board. Always a hard worker, so he was a good deal for those farms where he worked. At the end of it Kamstra took an agricultural exam which he passed easily. Now he was ready to apply for that coveted visa, his ticket into Canada.

He headed to the Canadian consulate in The Hague, where he was given a medical assessment and interview. At 24 years of age, he was the epitome of strength and good health. Surely, Canada would want such a fine specimen—and they did. The visa was pasted into his passport.

Tjebbe's new sweetheart, Jantje Dilling, whom he had met at Warffum during his first farm internship, had intended to emigrate with Tjebbe but instead decided to remain in Holland for a year then join him once he was established. His family grew fond of this girl; she was talkative, friendly, and pretty too. When the day of departure arrived—April 20, 1954—Sietse and Jantje accompanied Tjebbe to the port in Rotterdam and bade him a tearful goodbye as he boarded the great ship, called the *"Groote Beer"* (Big Bear). This ocean liner carried Tjebbe and more than 800 other hopeful Dutch immigrants across the Atlantic to the Canadian shore.

Groote Beer was originally a military troop carrier owned by the Dutch government that was converted into a passenger liner. The government owned three such ships, all run by the Holland America Line employed in the service of transporting emigrants from Holland to North America. The ship averaged thirteen such voyages a year from 1951 to 1962, mostly running back and forth between the Netherlands and Canada. It also made several trips to the United States and Australia.

The Netherlands encouraged emigration and even financially assisted many to cover the cost of the voyage. After the war, the Netherlands was in a depressed economic state for many years. Jobs were limited or poor paying and there were so many people living in such a small land area. In 1950 the country supported a population of ten million inhabitants on a territory of about 40,000 square kilometres making it one of the most densely populated countries on Earth. Meanwhile, immense, sparsely inhabited countries like Canada and Australia were eager to boost their populations with skilled or unskilled labourers and especially entrepreneurs. Hundreds of thousands ventured abroad to make their way in a new land, and Tjebbe was one of them. Most of those who left were young, not yet established, including singles, newlyweds, and new families.

Groote Beer sailed out in calm weather heading out from Rotterdam through the sheltered waters of the English Channel. Ship life was good, passengers were treated well. Food was exquisitely prepared, served in abundance and variety. There was entertainment on board, a live band and dances in the evening.

On the second day of the voyage, once on the open sea, the winds picked up and the amplitude of the swells increased. The sky darkened, rain pelted down, and the wind howled. It soon developed into a full-blown storm. Great rolls of moving water made the ship rock up and down, and pitch side to side. Waves crashed over and onto the deck. Most passengers confined themselves to their quarters, many with their heads over toilets as they expelled their previous meals. Tjebbe had a strong stomach and good sea legs developed from his days in the merchant marine. From then on there were calmer days and rougher days but none as bad as that first storm of April 22.

On the seventh day, a sliver of land appeared on the horizon. It was Canada. First to appear was the irregular rocky terrain of Newfoundland. A day later, on April 28th, the ship docked at Pier 21, Halifax, Nova Scotia. Pier 21 was an ocean liner terminal and immigration processing facility, the main entry point for immigrants coming into Canada during the 1950s. Pier 21 operated from 1928 until 1971, providing the gateway for over a million immigrants who nearly all arrived by sea over that period. Many thousands of Dutch pushed their way through these gates during the 1950s. Others originated from other lands: especially England, Germany, and Italy.

Customs forms had to be filled in upon arrival and immigration papers had to be in order. People debarked from *Groote Beer* and formed a long line that took hours to process. All clothing on person and in luggage had to be disinfected. Uniformed customs officers carefully scrutinized all passports and entry visas. Tjebbe was welcomed into Canada.

Once through the red tape of customs at this port of entry, most of the Dutch migrants made their way to the adjacent train station. They were on their way to destinations much further west, into the interior of this vast country. Tjebbe, however, was going no further, he would make his claim in Nova Scotia.

Jantje never did leave the Netherlands. It is not known if Tjebbe ever wrote her a letter or if he really had the intention of sending for her, but they never saw each other again. Sietse ran into Jantje on the street in Meppel a few years later. He called her name and tried to make conversation. She would not look him in the eye or even acknowledge that she knew him. Jantje just turned and walked away, saying nothing. Tjebbe must have broken her heart, too.

CHAPTER 5

Taking a New Name in Nova Scotia

Customs complete, Tjebbe grabbed his suitcases and passed through the bureaucratic gate. This was Canada! He saw a couple of waving hands stick up in the waiting crowd, then saw the familiar faces of Harmen and his wife, Roeli. He had not seen his beloved brother in four years. After hugs and handshakes, they made for the station to catch a train bound for Windsor, about 60 kilometres from Halifax on the Bay of Fundy side of the province. Tjebbe checked into a hotel in Windsor while Harmen and Roeli continued on to the Annapolis Valley where they lived.

Next morning Tjebbe ventured out to explore his new surroundings and to try figure out what he could do. Windsor seemed a pleasant little town, but for first impressions, Tjebbe found Nova Scotia a bit disappointing. It was a rough country, places were unkempt, and more rustic than what he was used to in his homeland. People didn't seem to take much pride in looking after their land. The terrain was undulating, much of it poor, rocky ground covered by scraggly trees.

The climate was harsh, he noted. The Netherlands would be in full spring by this time of year with flowers blooming and trees leafed out. Here the land was barely out of winter. It must be a difficult place to farm. Much of the land was vacant, not being used by people at all. He noticed a farm with a greenhouse on the edge of town; now that was something he could relate to. Tjebbe went in to look for the owner. He knocked several times before an elderly man of about eighty answered the door. The chap appeared friendly enough and he introduced himself as Charlie McClelland. Tjebbe returned the introduction and said that he was "just off the boat" and looking for work. Why yes, Charlie could use some help with running the greenhouse, so he hired the fit looking young man on the spot.

The greenhouse boiler was a full-sized train locomotive that pumped and pushed hot water through metal pipes to provide heat for the plants when the weather was cold. Walter and Mabel Davidson were an amiable couple in their forties who also worked in Charlie's greenhouse. Walter instructed Tjebbe on the idiosyncrasies of operating the locomotive engine, quite different from any boiler he had worked on before. The attentive Dutchman with a good sense of mechanics caught on quickly.

Cucumbers and tomatoes grew in the greenhouse which greatly extended the short Nova Scotia growing season. Several beehives needed tending. Tjebbe was soon doing a bit of everything around the farm: maintaining the boiler, planting, weeding, harvesting various fruits, and making repairs on buildings or equipment as necessary. Tjebbe paid a visit to the Justice of the Peace in town to apply for a licence so he could legally drive vehicles on the farm. Old McClelland was getting frail and could no longer trust himself behind the wheel. Tjebbe would chauffeur him around town to get supplies, or to Halifax, or any other destination as needed. The variety of farm work suited him. He impressed the old man and developed a close relationship with him. Charlie had an estranged son who he had very little contact with. Perhaps that was why he started treating Tjebbe like a son.

Charlie McClelland owned a second clapboard house on his property which he rented out to a woman with a ragtag collection of children of various sizes. One day as the children played in the yard, a swarm of bees streamed out from one of Charlie's hives. If a second queen bee develops within a hive, part of the colony leaves en masse with the new queen looking for a new site. The swarm descended on the head of a six-year-old boy. He screamed frantically as the buzzing mass of insects crawled over his face and hair. Charlie, alerted to the commotion by the screaming, ran over, picked up the flailing child, and carried him into the cellar of the house. Once in the dark the bees calmed down. Charlie carefully coaxed the living cluster off the boy and into a bucket. The boy calmed down, too. Thanks to Charlie's quick thinking and knowledge of bee behaviour, the boy did not suffer a single sting.

Tjebbe took room and board with Walter and Mabel in their farmhouse. They had no children so there was plenty of room. Since Charlie had lost his wife, he too lived with the Davidsons. It was a convenient arrangement. Mabel was so amiable and easy to talk to and glad for the company. Tjebbe was happy to reciprocate by lending a strong hand around the house whenever a chore needed to be done. One day as their conversation wandered from one topic to another Mabel brought up the question of his name.

"I never met anyone with a name like yours before," she said. "It is hard to pronounce or spell or even remember. Did you ever think of changing your name to something more, well, Canadian?"

Tjebbe had not but now he questioned how many others had thought the same. Would he always be considered an outsider because he had a strange name? What the heck, a name is just a name. He would change it if that would make it easier for Canadians. But what should he call himself? He rolled over a few possibilities then settled on "Jim," it had the "J" of "Tjebbe" and "Jim" was the colloquial form of the more formal English name "James." From then on, he would introduce himself as Jim Kamstra. And from herein in the story, he will be referred to as "Jim."

His biggest concern about the name change was what his mother would think. He was, after all, named after her father, Tjebbe Dykstra. Pietje did feel hurt when she first found out but accepted it if that is what he wanted. Of course, he would always be "Tjebbe" to her and she would call him nothing else.

His name was not the only thing that Jim changed in an effort to Canadianize himself. His English was passable, but he knew his accent was strong, so he sought out a way to improve it. He learned of a retired teacher in nearby Falmouth, Miss Hyde, who taught English in the evenings. Jim was an eager student who set his mind to the task, and soon gained full command of the language. His accent softened but did not disappear. When he spoke, he would always be recognized as a Dutchman.

When Jim longed for something familiarly Dutch, he would visit with Harmen and Roeli in the Annapolis Valley whenever he could. Roeli's parents and sister, Ali, also immigrated to Nova Scotia and they all lived together. It was a happy household with occasional parties and lots of music. One sister played the piano and the other an accordion. At get-togethers, everyone belted out the words of familiar Dutch songs. These were happy times. On a few occasions, the two brothers met up to fish in one of the salmon rich rivers or visit local sites.

One day, his ex-girlfriend Karin Bowman, the former secretary to the baroness, appeared at his door. Jim had not written to her so

Professional Photo of Harmen and Jim that they had made to send to their mother.

how did she find him here? The poor girl was lovesick for the man she knew as Tjebbe. She made the move to Nova Scotia just to be near him, desperately hoping to rekindle the relationship. Whatever Jim felt for her once, he no longer did, and he told her as much. Nonetheless she clung on to hope and kept tabs on Jim for a time. Eventually it was clear that the stubborn man was not going to be won over. Heartbroken she gave up. Where she went from there Jim never knew; he never saw her again.

In September 1954, Hurricane Edna moved north along the east coast, striking Nova Scotia with a vengeance. Winds up to 160 kilometres per hour were recorded in Yarmouth. Destruction was widespread, sections of forest were flattened, numerous buildings collapsed, roads washed out, powerlines downed, and hydro was out across the province for days. The McClelland farm too sustained severe damages. Jim had never witnessed such a catastrophic force of nature. The crops were destroyed, the greenhouse glass smashed with broken shards scattered across the yard, and the boiler was busted.

Charlie was devastated. He didn't know what to do or how he was ever going to recover at this stage in his life. He was unable to keep Jim employed on the farm. Jim felt bad but what could he do? He wanted to help, but Charlie told him to go. No one else would be hiring in Windsor now, so there was not much point in staying. With a solemn handshake, Jim bade farewell to the white-haired man who had been so good to him.

Harmen had a contract growing chrysanthemums for a wealthy man in Halifax, and he suggested that Jim contact him for possible employment. William D. Piercey was a well-known and respected entrepreneur. He owned Piercey Supplies, a Nova Scotia lumber company, as well as Piercey Investors and he had other business interests including real estate. He had even developed an area of Halifax known as Dutch Village, although he was not Dutch. Piercey was now an elderly man in his late seventies, so he no longer felt adept at negotiating the Halifax traffic and tortuous Nova Scotia roads. Jim became the personal chauffer not only for W.D., as he liked to be called, but also for his wife, Annie. Whenever they wanted or needed to go somewhere, W.D would say, "Jimmy, let's go."

Mr. Piercey was profoundly Christian, so loved to talk about the Bible when he sat in the passenger seat. Jim had no choice but to listen, but thanks to his father he was familiar enough with the good book that he could carry on meaningful conversation on the subject. The Pierceys had a stately home with a spacious lawn and large flower gardens that needed the hands of a gardener. This was well within Jim's capabilities; he got to dig in the soil and work with plants again.

As winter approached, however, the garden plants became dormant so there was not much to do. Jim went to work in Piercey's sawmill earning 85 cents per hour for sixty hours a week, a little better than he could earn on the farm during the slow winter. Lumber had to be cut, sorted, and stacked. The constant grinding and high decibels of the circular saw as it sliced lumber was numbing and made for long days. Winter set in and temperatures dropped. Some days it turned bitterly cold, considerably colder than the moderated Dutch winters that Jim was used to. And snow, so much snow, often a metre deep or more. He'd never seen anything like it. Just walking through that white stuff was tricky when it got that deep. The mill was not heated and much of the work was outside so there was no getting away from it. He needed better clothes for his new frigid country.

It was clear that Atlantic Canada was not the land of opportunity that Jim was hoping for. The Nova Scotia economy was not very rosy in the 1950s. He had heard the rumours of a better place, where labour was in great demand and wages higher. One just needed to make it to the heartland: the great province of Ontario to the west. But it was so far away, like going from the Netherlands to Ukraine.

From time-to-time, Jim visited his cousin, Ellie Haagsma—a daughter of Bauke's sister, Geert—who had also immigrated to Halifax. Ellie's boyfriend talked about a Dutch tobacco farmer that he knew in Ontario, John Hooyer, who often needed workers on his farm. Jim wrote an inquiry letter to that man and was pleased to receive a prompt reply with a promise of employment. Even better, Hooyer connected Jim to another Maritimer who was planning to drive to Toronto and was seeking company and someone to share expenses for the long trip.

After toughing it out through the bone-chilling winter of '55, Jim resigned from Piercey Supplies. W.D. was not happy to lose such a fine chauffeur, gardener, and general handyman, but he understood that such a man needs to make his own way in the world. In April 1955, Jim jumped into the car of his westbound acquaintance. He tossed in a suitcase containing his meagre belongings and headed out of the Maritimes.

CHAPTER 6

Ontario, the Place to Be

Never had Jim been on such a long drive. They followed winding roads through the forested hills of New Brunswick, then along straighter highways through the St. Lawrence lowlands of French-speaking Quebec, a province bigger than any European country. After three days on the road, sharing stories of women and life's lessons, his driving companion dropped Jim off at a hotel in Oshawa, Ontario. The driver carried on to Toronto.

Next day Jim hired a taxi to take him to John Hooyer's tobacco farm in the sandy hill country near Nestleton. John greeted his new employee with a firm, friendly handshake, pleased to see that determined look in his eye. Jim's first job was to install an oil-fired steam boiler and the associated piping that would provide a heating system into a series of tobacco kilns. A kiln is a simple square wooden building with a steep-sloped roof where the tobacco leaves are hung on layered slats to dry.

The warm summer air does a reasonable job drying, but a heater will speed up the process, particularly during humid or cool periods. Also, the boiler could be adjusted to pump steam into the kilns if the tobacco became too dry and brittle. The tobacco had to be cured just right. If dried too fast the fuzzy leaves would get crispy and if too slow, they could develop mould. Jim would learn the subtleties of this delicate process. With that job complete John took Jim to his other tobacco farm near Pontypool, about 20 kilometres away, to install another steam boiler system.

Nestleton was a rural farming village where neighbours all knew each other's business. Fortunately, Jim did not have to stay there but was able to secure room and board with the Hooyer family farmhouse where his two daughters and a son also resided. The shapely eldest daughter, Jocie, did not escape Jim's notice. Jim was given free use of Hooyer's pickup truck, so he asked Jocie out to a dance in the nearby town of Port Perry. She accepted and was impressed with Jim's moves on the dancefloor.

"Where did you learn to dance like that?" she asked.

"Why it's just what us Dutchmen do," he replied.

Was John concerned about his daughter dating the hired hand? If so, better that he was out of the house and further away. After a few months with the Hooyer family, Jim moved back to the Pontypool farm and the relationship went no further. At the farm, Jim worked in the crop, picking the tobacco and carefully hanging it up in the kilns.

Picking tobacco was back breaking and tedious. Only a couple of lower leaves would be picked from any plant, then the picker moved on to the next. The leaves were placed on a wagon and later would be hung and spaced out on racks in the kiln. Once the velvety leaves were dried, they had to be baled. Jim didn't mind working in the hot sun but handling tobacco was not pleasant. Workers wore no gloves. After an hour or so of picking, a black, tarry substance would coat the hands and forearms. The stuff was tacky on the skin as well as itchy. At each day's end Jim had to scrub vigorously to wash it off.

Later he learned that the coating contained nicotine, rumoured to be a serious health hazard. Jim was not too concerned about such things. Although smoking was popular among men at the time, Jim did not smoke much. John Hooyer told him one day, "If you work in tobacco you've got to smoke like a man." Jim picked up the habit to fit in and support the industry that he now worked in.

Tobacco was one of the most lucrative crops that a farmer could grow and it also paid fair wages to anyone working it. After a couple of months, Jim was able to stash away $2000, enough to buy a brand-new car. True to the Dutch stereotype Jim was no spendthrift, however. He worked hard for his money and therefore did not spend it lavishly. But tobacco growing was only a seasonal occupation. As summer transformed into autumn the work dried up so he would have to find something else.

Jim often corresponded about his new life with his mother through letters. He told her about his exciting experiences, leaving out the details of anything that a mother shouldn't know. Pietje, so eager to hear from her beloved Tjebbe, wrote back with news of the happenings at home. He missed his mother. If he experienced any homesickness however, he would not admit it, not even to himself. She mentioned that one of their Meppel neighbours, John Sierhuis had emigrated and now lived in Oshawa. Jim knew John well enough, so he decided to get in touch.

"You must come over a visit and a *lekker* Dutch meal," coaxed John.

Jim could hardly refuse that offer so he made his way to the Sierhuis family home on Darlington Blvd. John had a spare bedroom in the basement apartment which he offered to Jim. What's more, John was an inspector on the assembly line at General Motors, the great automobile manufacturer. Now that was a place where one could earn serious good wages, with benefits too. Maybe John could help him get hired. Jim submitted a job application, but the plant was on strike in autumn 1955.

General Motors, referred by everyone as 'GM', was by far the biggest employer in Oshawa, dominating the local economy. If GM shut down much of the townsfolk were out of work and therefore not spending money. Restaurants, clothing stores, and many other establishments suffered. It was not a good time to be job hunting, but he had to try! Jim visited various other factories and establishments looking for work, not only in Oshawa but as far away as Port Hope, well to the east.

Finally, a company called Kitchen Installations offered him employment. Since the factory was located 25 kilometres to the west, Jim needed an automobile. He purchased his very first, a brand-new Vauxhall for $1500, paid in full with cash. Now he really felt like a man, windows rolled down as he cruised through town in his own set of wheels. Kitchen Installations was no slack job. He buffered brand new sinks and was paid on piecework. That suited him fine since he worked faster than most others and was able to take home a reasonable paycheck. Jim knew this was not a long-term career and the long drive was irritating.

The GM strike was settled, and the company was hiring more staff since they were now backlogged after the long factory closure. Jim was taken on to do general maintenance in the plant. This entailed a variety of tasks such as simple repairs, carpentry, and cutting frames with a blow torch. Something different every day. He was there for nearly half a year when administration moved him onto the assembly line, installing drive shafts into automobile frames.

He felt like a robot on the assembly line. It was tedious, repetitive and monotonous. Most workers were contented to work the line because the pay was so good, but Jim knew that this job would suck the life out of him if he stayed at it too long. The boss must have seen this for Jim was called into the office one day for a chat. Jim was soon reassigned as a gardener and general handyman to look after the grounds around the General Motors plant. He would be outside cutting grass, tending to flower beds and trimming bushes. In winter, he moved inside to cleanup offices on the night shift. This was easy work but not very satisfying for the ambitious man.

CHAPTER 7

The Woman of His Dreams

The ruggedly handsome hard-working Dutchman had met several young ladies and had been out on various dates since coming to Canada. None had thus far been the "right one," so he kept playing the field. Then one evening Jim attended a meeting of a Dutch Canadian acting group at the Ukrainian Hall in Oshawa to find out what that was about. He could not help but notice an attractive buxom brunette sitting on a nearby bench, but he did not approach or talk to her. A week or so later while walking along a city sidewalk, Jim saw the same brunette walking towards him, then she passed him on the side. He turned around for just a second, and so did she, a smile on her face.

What a fine-looking lass, he thought. They both continued walking in opposite directions.

One fateful evening in the spring of 1956 Jim attended a singles dance for new immigrants held at Adelaide House on Simcoe Street in Oshawa. Adelaide House's main purpose was to provide refuge for single women, but it also had a dance floor in the basement. Many Dutch, as well as British, Germans, Italians and other new immigrants came out to enjoy themselves. In the decorated hall a disk jockey played an assortment of dance music: tangos, foxtrots, swing, and the like. Jim glanced around the crowd to see if there was anyone he recognized.

And there she was, that brunette again! It must be fate. Then he bumped into a new acquaintance, Ralph de Boo Van Uiein and his date. They shared a drink and small talk. What luck—Ralph's girlfriend was a friend of the brunette, so she made the introductions. Corry Huitenga was her name. Jim asked her to dance, and she followed him to the floor. Corry moved in time to Jim's lead. She had also taken lessons in the old country. They just floated across the floor as one dance led to another, making small talk in between. At the

Corry Huitenga, the apple of Jim's eye.

end of the night, Jim asked if he could drive her home and Corry agreed.

Corry was born and raised in the town of Franeker in Friesland province, only 80 kilometres from Meppel. She had also crossed the Atlantic on the *Groote Beer*, the same ship that carried Jim, but a year later. She was staying with her eldest sister, Aggie, and Aggie's farmer husband, Walter Pieterse, in a farmhouse a few kilometres east of Oshawa.

Aggie and Walter married in the Netherlands in 1951 then emigrated as newlyweds. They had two small children, John and Celia. Unlike Aggie, Corry did not intend to make Canada her home. She planned to stay for a year just to get a taste of life in a different country, make a little money, then return to her beloved Netherlands. After surviving several months in this relatively unsophisticated place she was not impressed with the land or its people. She found both to be rustic and unrefined. Her homeland was familiar, with a long history and culture; her friends and most of her close-knit family were there.

A week later, the phone rang in the Pieterse's kitchen. It was Jim asking to speak to Corry, eager to go on a real date. She was all he could think about ever since the dance. Aggie was suspicious of this eager young man courting her little sister and said so before handing her the phone.

"Corry, this fellow may be Dutch, but he is not a Catholic," she warned. "Best to stick to our own kind".

Corry did not heed her advice; she was just enjoying the man's attention and knew she would only be around for a year anyway. One date led to another, however.

They could almost be considered a couple when Jim offered to teach Corry how to drive a car. She hopped into the four-speed Vauxhall and they set off on a drive to Peterborough. Jim described the basics of driving: the instrument panel, the sequence of gear shifting, how to alternate footwork between clutch, throttle and brake, and what to watch out for on the road. It was Corry's first time behind the wheel. She was nervous and very cautious. Patience was not Jim's strongest point and his critical approach to giving instructions didn't help.

"Let up the clutch slowly until it grabs, slowly, slowly... Oh, you stalled it again!" he barked. Since Jim caught on to new tasks quickly, he expected that others could do the same.

Corry was starting to get it and was moving along slowly. So much to keep track of she thought: brake, clutch, gas, stick shift, rear-view mirror, not to mention keeping eyes on the road.

Wham!

The Vauxhall rammed into the back of another car. It was not a hard hit but there was minor damage to both vehicles — a warped grill, a bent bumper, and busted taillights. Jim reacted explosively with a burst of Dutch profanity.

She did not take it well. On the way home Corry suggested they should break up. Her being Catholic and Jim a not very devout protestant was not likely to work out well anyway.

"Fine, Corry," he replied, "but you owe me some money for the accident and damages to fix up the car."

"Alright, then!"

That was that.

Jim and Corry's wedding day. Corry's sister Gina was Maid of Honour and Harry Van Alebeck was Best Man.

Attendees at the wedding. To the right of Jim: Gina, Paul Ten Westeneind, Aggie and Walter Pieterse. The children in front are Celia and John Pieterse.

But Jim could not stay away. He dropped in on Corry a couple of weeks later with the invoice for car damages. While there, he asked her out to a movie. She accepted and off they went. Before long the two were going out regularly again. Corry tried not to get too stuck on this man in motion, for she was committed to returning to her homeland by year's end — but Jim was smitten. He asked Corry out at every opportunity to dances, movies, or out with friends. He knew he would have to turn up the charm to keep her in Canada.

It was not long before Corry had to admit she was falling for this energetic wavy-haired fellow. Yes, they shared a Dutch bond, but there was so much more. Jim could tell stories and keep Corry laughing. A social drink now and then didn't hurt either.

Later that spring, Gina, another of Corrie's sisters, abandoned Holland for Canada. Once she arrived Corry left the Pieterse family to share an apartment with Gina in Oshawa. Another attractive Huitenga gal, Gina also had her male pursuers and soon she found her own dynamic Dutchman, Paul Ten Westeneind.

"At least he is a Catholic!" Aggie remarked.

The sisters were tight, Gina was only two years older than Corrie. Before long, Jim was getting to know Paul. The gents found that they had more in common than an attraction to Huitengas. They shared many character traits including a propensity to socialize, a general outlook on life, and love for fishing. Soon Paul and Jim were also tight, and it all felt so natural. What luck when siblings and their partners click.

Jim knew that Corry was the one for him. There was never a doubt. He proposed to her. It was only four months after they had met. Jim's choice of words was "it is time I put my feet under my own table."

She accepted.

One slight problem though, the religious differences. She was quite a devout Roman Catholic while he was a lacklustre Protestant, but he loved her so much that he enrolled in a course to convert to Catholicism. He sat and participated in the weekly lessons at St. Gregory's Church for three months, but unlike the others, he did not convert at the end of it. Nevertheless, it gave him the credentials he needed to be able to wed in a Catholic church, and this was important to Corry. They also committed to raising whatever children they might have in the Catholic faith. Some of his friends urged Jim to make the

Catholic transition but it just did not feel right. If Corry was disappointed, she never let him know.

Some of Jim's workmates at General Motors were a crude bunch of characters. One of the unsavoury traditions at the motors was to "blackball" a man just before he was about to get married. A group of workers would corner and capture the soon-to-be groom, holding him down. Someone else would pull down his pants while another would smear axle grease or even paint around his penis and testicles, creating a disgusting mess and a most unpleasant nuptial night.

Jim was wise to this nasty prank so was wary when in the washroom. Nevertheless, a gang of fellow workers found their moment, grabbed him, and pinned him down. Jim struggled to break free from these hoodlums, but there were too many so he yelled out as loud as he could. Luckily the foreman heard the commotion, charged into the washroom, then hollered at the men to break it up, sparing Jim from the injustice.

The sun shone brightly on the afternoon of September 22, 1956. Jim and Corry were married in the gothic hall of St. Gregory's Church in Oshawa, by Father Paul Dwyer. The best man was Harry Van Alebeck (husband of one of Corry's friends) while the maid of honour was Corry's sister, Gina. The whole crowd attending their wedding consisted of a mere twenty people including the Pieterse family, Paul Ten Westeneind, Gina, and Piet Witjes. No parents came from Netherlands and there were no relatives on the Kamstra side. Perhaps just as well for neither Jim's nor Corry's parents approved of the wedding, on account of the religious differences. After the formal church ceremony, the wedding group gathered at the house on Ritson Road South, where Jim was boarding. Wedding photos were taken on the step of that house.

Jim rented a red car for the ceremony. After the dinner and dancing, the newlyweds sped away from the wedding party, driving east to spend their nuptial night at a motel in the village of Welcome, near Port Hope. From there the honeymoon was a whirlwind weeklong tour of the eastern reaches of Ontario: Picton, Kingston, the Thousand Islands, La Chine, Montreal, Algonquin Park, Huntsville and then back to Oshawa. Corry would not be returning to the Netherlands now.

CHAPTER 8

Time to Start a Family

Once the dreamy honeymoon was over Jim and Corry got down to the serious business of making a new life together. Their first home was an upstairs apartment at 30 Athol Street in Oshawa. It was a blissful time, just the two of them. Love was new and life was fresh and simple.

When their landlady jacked up the rent, they moved out to another upstairs apartment on Conlin Road, north of the city. It consisted of just two rooms, a kitchen/living room and a bathroom. Their bed had to be folded up in the day to give them room to move about. Both Jim and Corry worked at General Motors through this period, trying to stash away as much cash as they could.

Although they loved their adopted country (at least Corry was learning to love it), they were not committed to staying in Oshawa. They talked about moving further west.

"Let's go to British Columbia," suggested Jim.

They both savoured that idea. Spectacular scenery, mountains, big trees, and milder winters. Many Dutch people had moved out there already. They were beginning to plan the westbound exodus, but an unplanned circumstance would change things. They were not using any form of birth control and Corry became pregnant within a few months of the wedding. Travelling in an advanced stage of pregnancy was unthinkable. They could not leave Ontario now and never would.

Corry's working days in the factory were also numbered. She quit work and prepared for the arrival of the baby. She had to find a crib, set up a nursery, and buy clothes for the newborn. Corry's girth increased as her mobility decreased. She found the later stages of pregnancy unbearable in the midsummer heat as no one had air conditioning. When she thought she could take no more, her water broke.

Time to go! Jim drove Corry to Oshawa General Hospital where she was rushed in to a delivery room. Jim paced and waited, thinking about how their lives would change then sat down in a reception area.

Fathers were not allowed in the birthing room so there was little to do. Their bundle of joy came into the world on schedule on August 23, 1957. It was a boy, and they named him Jamie, or formally James, after his father.

Soon after delivery, the newborns were taken from their mothers for a brief period. They would be cleaned up then lined up in a display window near the waiting room, for fathers and other onlookers to admire. Jim peered into the window at four tiny pink wrinkly newborns. Although they were not labelled, Jim immediately knew which one had to be his. Only one baby had a prominent notch in the brow above his nose, a distinctive Kamstra trait. When the babies were returned to their mothers, Corry saw that the nurse was about to place the "notched" baby into the arms of another new mother who shared the room.

"Hey, hey, that baby is mine!" Corry called out sternly.

"Oops, okay, terribly sorry," said the tired nurse.

The young Kamstra family soon moved to Courtice on Highway 2, occupying the same house where Corry had lived with her sister Aggie and the rest of the Pieterse family. Walter had purchased his own farm near Wainfleet in the Niagara Peninsula. They moved out, making their rustic house available for rent. It was a pretty basic bungalow, a shack really. In fact, before the Pieterses had moved in only a few years earlier, the building had been a gas station. The owner, Bill Walters, who lived across the road, converted it into a house so that it could be rented out.

The shack had no internal plumbing and no septic system. The toilet was a detached outhouse in the backyard, a wooden bench with a hole over a deep pit in the ground. On Halloween night some of the local boys pushed over the outhouse, a common prank at the time. The next day Jim had the task of resetting the wobbly structure.

To get water there was a cast-iron hand pump beside the kitchen sink that had to be cranked vigorously. Taking a bath entailed boiling water on the stove and pouring it into a metal tub. Any gray water from the sink drained out through a pipe to the ditch. As an improvement, Jim dug a hole which he filled with branches so that the gray water could percolate back into the ground. An oil-fired space heater provided warmth, but it was not very efficient and with thin insulation, the little house never got cozy in the winter. The oil that fed it came through a metal tube from an outside tank. The valve on the tank needed to be closed when the heater was turned off. Jim forgot to do this one morning and stove oil leaked in. By the time they noticed, the linoleum floor was covered; cleanup was a messy ordeal.

Walter had been growing a great number of gladiolus flowers in the back garden which he sold to local florists as cut flowers. When the Pieterses moved, they could not take that with them, so Jim purchased the whole lot, several thousand bulbs in all. He thought this venture would be a lucrative sideline project. The bulbs were stored in the basement over winter then planted out in rows in the spring. No small task. Jim vigorously dug up the beds and planted in evenings and on the weekend since he had a regular job. The plants grew tall then after three months sported long stalks of large petalled showy flowers in a variety of colours. Jim was able to sell many bunches to local florists but also went door to door through neighbourhoods to sell the cut flowers. Corry helped and they even carted along baby Jamie on their selling sprees. Perhaps the adorable infant attracted attention and helped them sell more flowers.

Living in the country had its moments. One night they could hear rustling and clanging from the tool shed that was attached to the side of the house. Next morning garbage cans were tipped over with rubbish scattered about. Obviously, an animal, but what kind? Jim was going to find out.

  The landlord stored tools, paint cans, and various other items in the shed. Jim found a metal leg-hold trap amongst the items and set it to catch the culprit. He attached the chain to an old rusty woodstove. That night Jim and Corry woke up to the sound of frantic shuffling, something was caught in the trap. Jim looked in to see a mostly black, cat-sized animal with a broad white stripe down its middle. It was a skunk, an animal unfamiliar to him.

  He grabbed his shotgun, opened the side door, took aim, and fired on the defenceless beast. Before dying, it did what skunks do, sprayed its potent juices every which way including toward Jim. The noxious fumes filled the shed and also penetrated the insides of the house. Corry was aghast. The pungent odour burned their nasal passages. Days later the smell was still strong. Getting advice from other people, they tried washing down the walls with tomato juice to little effect. Javex bleach worked a lot better but even that did not completely rid the house of that foul aroma. But on the bright side, Jim now knew what a skunk was and he would not do that again.

Corry`s sister Gina married Paul Ten Westeneind on the last day of December 1957, before a small gathering at the same church in Oshawa where Jim and Corry married a year earlier. Paul was already a Roman Catholic so that made things easier for them and their families. Corry was the maid of honour, wearing her own wedding dress which she dyed light blue. Piet Witjes filled the role of the best man.

Corry's parents, Jan and Cecilia Huitenga, came to visit in the summer of 1958. Three of their daughters were now living in Canada so the Huitengas divided their two-month visit between them, sometimes staying at the rustic homestead in rural Courtice. Jim had the distinct feeling that Jan was displeased with this poor excuse of a house that his daughter was living in, but he said nothing.

Then at the end of their stay, Jan said to Corry, "Jim is a good man, I like him very much. Too bad he is not Catholic."

Jim with Corry's parents Cecile and Jan Huitenga, Gina, Corry and Aggie Pieterse on an outing in Toronto.

Corry seemed to be happy with Jim, and although conditions were a little crude, this was her life now. However, Jim, Corry, and Jamie did not stay in the ramshackle house much longer. After a couple of years of hard work and saving, the frugal couple managed to put away enough cash to purchase a house, a home they could truly call their own. This house was also located on Highway 2, about three kilometres further west, closer to Oshawa. For the asking price of $10,000, the house was theirs.

This was a definite improvement, a real house with hot and cold running water, flush toilet, bathtub, and even a garage. It was a bungalow with three bedrooms. The backyard was narrow and fenced in, with neighbours on the east and west sides and adjacent vacant land along the back. They moved in the spring of 1959 when Corry's bulging belly indicated that another child was coming.

This house had issues too, however. As soon as they moved in, they found that water in the toilet would not drain; the septic pipes were clogged by coagulated sewage left by the previous tenants. Jim's first task after moving in consisted of scraping out the blobs of slimy odiferous material from the pipes. Instead of hiring a plumber Jim did the job himself. Corry also helped, despite the condition she was in.

Jim cutting the lawn assisted by 2-year old Jamie.

Corry was looking forward to her second child and convinced that this one would be a daughter. She was praying that it would be a girl. But that was not how the stars were aligned. On July 8, 1959, she gave birth to their second son, whom they named Harry John, after Jim's brother Harmen. Initially disappointed and somewhat depressed, Corry realized it was silly to put so much faith in something that was beyond her control and loved this boy as much as the first.

Corry was pregnant again within a year, with the anticipated due date in late January 1961. She had an agreement with Mrs. Tenking, a middle-aged Dutch woman who lived a few doors away. Mrs. Tenking would look after Jamie and Harry when Corry needed to go to the hospital to deliver. Soon after she had made the arrangement Corry started feeling contractions — but this was too soon. The baby wasn't due for another six weeks. Shocked, she called Mrs. Tenking to ask her to come right away.

"Okay I will come over when I have finished the cooking and cleaning", replied Mrs. Tenking.

Corry had to explain the urgency of the situation. Then she called Jim who was selling Christmas trees at Preston's Garage in north Oshawa. He rushed home, picked up Corry, and raced her to the Oshawa General Hospital just in time.

Theodore, boy number three, came into the world on December 13, 1960. He was named, after Corry's youngest brother, Theo. The tiny red-faced newborn was premature, weighing only five pounds. He was so frail and ill-equipped to deal with cold that he had to be confined to an incubator for his first weeks of life. Theodore developed healthily in his climate-controlled chamber and was able to come home in January. Corry had her hands full now raising a house of boys: washing cloth diapers as well as the rest of the laundry, cooking, cleaning, and keeping house. Thank God she now had a wringer washing machine and a vacuum cleaner to make life easier.

Perhaps because he had been born premature, Theodore showed no desire to walk by the time he was a year old, and he just would not talk. He was not reaching the milestones of other toddlers. Occasionally he would spew out a few slurred words, especially when getting excited while playing with his brothers. The concerned parents felt they had better intervene.

At age four, Theodore was taken to weekly sessions with a speech therapist who worked on his enunciation and confidence. He was still a little awkward when he started kindergarten but perhaps through interacting with teachers and peers, he developed confidence and soon spoke like any normal five-year-old.

The three sons: Theodore, Jamie and Harry in 1963.

There was a lot going on in and around the little house on Highway 2. For a short while, Albert Tenking, a butcher, rented the sunken garage to prepare, store, and sell meat to customers. It was a very small operation and he eventually moved his equipment out. Then Jim found a new use for the garage. He acquired an old wooden sailboat that had seen better days. He hauled it into the garage, turning it into a sailboat repair shop. The winter project was to fix up the old skiff making it sea-worthy again.

Jim learned as he went, replacing planks, sanding, applying fibreglass to the hull, repairing the sail, shellacking the mast, painting the trim. By spring it was finished. He loaded the craft on a trailer, then drove it to nearby Lake Ontario. The family climbed aboard, Jim hoisted up the sails, and the wind took them away. It moved marvellously through the waves. After such a labour of love, Jim only sailed the boat a few times before selling it.

Then one day without warning, Harmen appeared at the door, having driven in from the East Coast. He came for a visit and asked if he could stay with them for a while. Although he was not forthcoming about his true situation, Harmen finally admitted that he had left his wife and three children in Nova Scotia, with no intention of returning. Jim and Corry were both annoyed and disappointed since they were very fond of Roeli and knew that she would have a rough time on her own. But Harmen was family, so they took him in. With no spare rooms in the house, they made some space and fixed up a bed in the garage.

Not wanting to overstay his welcome Harmen, found his own apartment in Oshawa a month later and moved out. Nevertheless, he frequently dropped in his brother's family during this period. One day Harmen pulled into the driveway behind the wheel of a sleek red convertible sports car with the top down. Jamie and Harry were impressed and thought their dapper uncle, who they called Uncle Harry, must be wealthy to own such a car. They even started referring to him as "Uncle Harry the Millionaire." Jim found this very amusing for he knew that his brother's financial resources were very limited. Fortunately for Harmen, Jim had connections with a manager at General Motors, who was able to get Harmen a job on the assembly line where he would stay for most of his working life.

CHAPTER 9

Landscaping — A New Career

Jim continued to work at General Motors for the first two years of marriage. During a winter snowstorm many workers did not make it into work but Jim, always dependable, still showed up. Exercising his authority, the foreman ordered Jim to complete some of the tasks normally done by others including cleaning toilets in both the men's and women's washrooms. Jim viewed this as a shameful task for a man.

"I did not come here to clean ladies' toilets," was Jim's response. "In fact, I have had enough. That's it! I quit."

The foreman was taken aback, surprised that Jim would react so strongly to this simple request. He recognized that Jim worked hard at whatever he did, so he did not want to lose such a valuable employee.

The foreman retracted. "Okay, forget it Jim, you don't have to bother with those washrooms, but can you do the rest?"

It was too late, however. Maybe this was just the excuse that he needed. When Jim said something, he meant it, whether a rash decision or not. He did not spend a lot of time pondering. This was a turning point. He was finished with GM but needed another job to support the family. He checked in at several establishments about town to see what he could find. One of those was Rundle's Garden Centre on King Street in Oshawa.

Albert Rundle, the kindly owner, offered him a job. Jim preferred outdoor work, and he liked being around plants. This was a welcome change from the assembly line or slack work in the GM plant. Instead of working in the centre, Albert sent him out to job sites, mostly private residences, to attend to whatever outside tasks that the customer requested. This could include planting trees, rolling out sod, cutting grass, laying patio slabs, tending to flowerbeds, pruning shrubs, spraying pesticides, installing retaining walls, and more.

Jack Janssen, another recent immigrant who Jim had met through Paul Ten Westeneind, was hunting for work at the time. Jim brought his good name forward to Albert, who did not have to think long before hiring him. Jack was an equally strong-willed, hardworking, wavy-haired Dutchman with a prominent nose. The two men found they had much in common, and anyone looking at them could have mistaken them for brothers.

Albert often sent Jim and Jack out together on various jobs, impressed at how they could work. They became a team, getting into a rhythm, each one attacking their respective tasks and efficiently getting the job done. They learned from, and also competed with each other, one trying to outwork the other. Albert was as fair a boss as one could hope for, however, they felt that he had an out-dated approach to landscaping. Each day involved heavy manual labour, shovelling soil on the back of a pickup truck, digging by hand and pushing wheelbarrows. Times were changing, this business should get more mechanized; they should be using tractors and bigger trucks, which would bring in greater profits. Albert, however, preferred to carry on the old way.

The ambitious young men had toiled on many projects but perhaps the most memorable was at Seven Mile Island on Lake Scugog. The 10-hectare island was owned by Mr. Patrick Harrison who purchased it in 1958 with big plans. Seven Mile Island had a long history of ownership by a series of wealthy owners going back to the 1880s. Alex Ross Wilson who bought the island in 1919 created an elaborate and highly manicured estate there with a 26 room mansion, reflecting pools, a rose garden, a water tower and arched walkways. It had been the fanciest piece of real estate on Lake Scugog for decades. However, times changed, Wilson died, and the family sold off the island. Although lived in by others, the gardens and buildings were not maintained and eventually were no longer being used. The estate had laid vacant for years and was in a state of disrepair when Harrison acquired it. He would invest over $1 million restoring and returning the grounds to their former splendour.

Seven Mile Island become a big project for Jack and Jim. They restored the showpiece rose gardens, which entailed planting hundreds of the thorny plants. Trellises were repaired, walkways levelled, and many trees and shrubs planted to Harrison's specifications. On one occasion dozens of dead muskellunge had washed up along the shoreline, accompanied by the overpowering aroma of decomposition. It was up to the two men to deal with this mess before it got worse. They scooped up the fish corpses onto a pickup truck and carted them off to the dump. The estate work kept them occupied, off and on, for over a year. When completed it looked grand, a showpiece they could be proud of. The project started as a Rundle Garden Centre contract, but partway along Janssen and Kamstra took over the job when they created their own independent company.

Seven Mile Island may have been the catalyst, but as they toiled and talked the over-ambitious Dutchmen thought about their future.

"How much profit is Albert making on our hard work?" Jim asked Jack. "If we worked for ourselves that profit would be in our pockets!"

In 1959, Jack and Jim resigned from Rundles and together formed a business partnership they would register as *Oshawa Home Landscaping*. Jim came up with the name.

"Oshawa is our town, and we landscape people's homes".
It made perfect sense.

They operated the business out of their personal properties. Jack had about an acre of land around his home at the end of Varcoe Road, just east of Oshawa. Here they cleared off a piece of the lot to create a work yard. They erected a shed where they could park the trucks and tractor, store a few supplies and keep the tools of the trade. Jim set up an office in his home on Highway 2, about a kilometre away. Corry looked after the bookkeeping, which involved documenting labour and materials of each job and sending out the invoices to customers once a month. Jack's wife Margaret showed little interest in the business; she found the noise of machinery and the dust it created around the house to be an annoyance.

Jack and Jim mostly worked on private residences, eagerly attending to a range of outside tasks. This mainly entailed planting and yard work but on occasion, they would install storm windows or fix leaky basements. Jim would visit customers at their homes in the evening, find out what they wanted, make a simple planting sketch for their approval to secure the next job. Neither men had any formal training in this line of work, they just figured things out as they went along. There were no certifications and few restrictions that applied to the landscape trade so they could pass themselves off as experts. As they gained experience, that is what they became, experts.

Some jobs required more finesse than others. Like the tricky business of installing a rock garden on the sloping terrain around the estate house at St. Gertrude's Church. Stones of various shapes and sizes had to be chosen carefully and placed to fit in the right spot on the hillside to achieve an artistic balance. Then they installed a combination of plant material that provided a natural look among the rock backdrop. Father Myers, who resided there, was pleased with the results.

In winter the ground froze and there was no demand for their services. Jim did not like being idle, so he found another way to keep bringing home some money. Brother-in-law Paul, now the owner of his own company, Western Electric, hired him on as an electrician's assistant for the colder months, helping install wires and sockets in houses under construction. With the first warm days of spring, Jim was glad to be back on the shovel.

Jack had a more aggressive approach to business than Jim, and he was willing to take bigger risks. He often pushed to acquire bigger equipment or apply for bigger contracts that Jim felt were beyond their capabilities. Jim was more cautious in this regard as he did not want to blow all the fruits of his labour on a bad business deal.

In one venture the two daring Dutchmen drove to Cleveland, Ohio with the intent of setting up a business to supply wholesale Christmas trees from Pontypool, Ontario. How did they come up with such an idea? Albert Jakely, the owner of the Oshawa Sod Supply had tried a similar scheme a few years earlier.

"There is a real demand for Canadian Christmas trees in Cleveland and they will pay a much higher price than you can get here," Jakely told them.

The possibility of doing business in the US was an adventure too good to pass. Jack and Jim had secured several deals with Ohio wholesale buyers, but then Jim found out that Albert had not been paid for some of his shipments and was out of pocket for a considerable sum of cash. Despite this news, Jack was still keen to pursue this questionable venture. Jim, however, was not. He insisted they turn it down.

Nevertheless, Oshawa Home Landscaping flourished. They hired on many workers, mostly European immigrants including Dutch, Germans, Hungarians, and Portuguese. At one point they employed about ten workers and owned several trucks. Janssen and Kamstra were an effective team for a time, there was a kind of synergy between them. There were some disagreements about what equipment to purchase or other business decisions, but they were mostly cooperative. Jack was not as frugal as Jim. The business was growing and the pace getting hectic, perhaps a little too hectic. Despite the apparent success that the company had achieved, the two decided it was time to go separate ways.

In 1962, the partnership was dissolved, and Oshawa Home Landscaping was no more. Years later Jim could not recall a particular incident that led to the breakup. Perhaps Jack was frustrated that Jim did not support his desire for bigger schemes. Maybe the two headstrong Dutchmen were just too similar and therefore did not complement each other. Margaret's disinterest in the business and often tumultuous relationship with Jack may have been a major factor in the breakup, Jim couldn't be sure. Jim sometimes wondered how far the business might have gone had they maintained the partnership. Perhaps they could have created an empire; perhaps it's just as well it ended when it did.

They parted as partners, but not as friends. Both men would continue in the landscaping business, so their customer list was split evenly. Then the equipment was divided with the flip of a coin. Jack would soon have a new operation. He bought King West Garden Centre, an existing company that was for sale at the west end of Oshawa. For a time, Jack and Jim were competitors in business. Then Jack had a desire to get out of Oshawa completely. He sold that business after a few years, moved north to Gravenhurst where he started Muskoka Landscaping. It would become a successful business in its own right.

CHAPTER 10

Partnership with Rundle

Neither Jim nor Corry had been back to the land of their birth since making a life in Canada. Most of their respective families remained in the old country. Their parents were ageing so they felt that it was time to pay a visit. In addition, they now had children to show off. It would be expensive, but they had saved up and could finally afford it.

In December 1961 Jack was good enough to drive the young family to Montreal International Airport, a ten hour round trip. They waited in the terminal for hours as the plane was delayed due to a snowstorm. Finally, onboard, the KLM Airlines DC-7 taxied around runways, ready for takeoff but then had to return to the airport for de-icing. Would this plane ever take off? Corry was stressed with three small children to contend with. Baby Theodore, lying on her lap, would not stop crying.

An annoyed passenger in the seat behind said, "Lady, can't you get that baby to be quiet?"

Corry, now at wit's end, turned around, held the baby out to them and exclaimed, "Here, you try it!"

The passenger didn't say anything more.

After a twelve-hour flight, they landed on familiar turf in Amsterdam. Corry's sister, Suus, and her husband, Herman, met them at the airport. With luggage and kids in tow, they hopped in the car which sped off to Franeker, Corry's hometown. Arriving at the home Corry grew up in, a welcoming party was waiting—parents, siblings, and neighbourhood friends all eager to see them. Jim and Corry had barely slept a wink the entire trip and were exhausted. They only wanted to sleep but the Huitenga relatives were so happy to see them that that was out of the question. The children were adored by their aunts, uncles, and especially, grandparents. For many it was the first time that they met Corry's husband. Her kid sister, Ria, was so impressed with her outgoing brother-in-law. If only she could find such a man for herself.

They needed to visit the Kamstra side also. Sietse, and his lovely blonde sweetheart, Wiesje Schuiling, had been going steady for five years. Jim approached his younger brother.

"So, when are you two going to marry?"

"Oh, I don't know, maybe in a year or so," replied Sietse.

"Why don't you do it while we are in the country?" Jim urged.

"Good idea."

Arrangements were put in motion. Their church minister was able to schedule a wedding on short notice and a hall was rented for the reception. Sietse and Wiesje married in a grand ceremony on January 22. Little Jamie was the ring bearer trailing behind the debonair couple as they strolled down the aisle. The marriage was announced so suddenly that many friends and relatives concluded that Wiesje must be pregnant!

While it was good to see their familiar childhood haunts and many of their loved ones, the old country was changing. Jim and Corry no longer felt a part of that land; they had wholeheartedly adopted Canada. Nevertheless, they would never abandon their Dutch heritage. Shortly after returning home, they decided to make it official.

Immigrants were required to reside in the country for at least five years before they could apply for Canadian Citizenship. The Kamstra couple filled out the appropriate forms that were sent to the federal government. They had to relinquish their Dutch citizenship however, as having dual was not an option then. A special ceremony was arranged at Oshawa City Hall for a whole gathering of new Canadians to be anointed as full-fledged citizens at the same time. Jim and Corry were eagerly awaiting the event, but a heavy blanket of snow fell on the city that day. Jim had a long list of snow cleaning contracts that he was responsible for. He set up the snowplow on his pickup truck and cleaned parking lots until the job was done. They missed the celebration but Judge Alex Hall, who presided over the procession, (and was also a customer) invited Jim and Corry to his home for a personal swearing-in ceremony.

Although officially Canadian, it was still easier to speak the mother tongue at home and when among their circle of Dutch friends. Jamie had grown up with Dutch and after the trip to Holland had a reasonable command of the language, as well as English, but he mixed words of both when he spoke. In September 1962, Jamie was enrolled in St.

Gertrude's Catholic School to attend kindergarten. To his teacher, Miss Liptay, and classmates, Jamie had a strange way of talking that they often could not understand. They could not grasp his unconventional form of English with a lot of Dutch words and grammar thrown in. The teacher needed to talk with the parents.

Jim and Corry then decided to stop speaking Dutch at home. Jim and Corry worked on improving their own command of the language by enrolling in English classes at night school. This had another advantage, for if Jim and Corry wanted to discuss sensitive topics that the children should not hear, they could revert to Dutch.

But still, the active and busy family needed more space. The little green and white bungalow on Highway 2 had become too small for the family of five. Jim felt that Corry and the kids deserved more. He purchased a half-acre lot on the Oshawa-Darlington Townline Road, less than a half kilometre to the west. An architect he knew drafted up a plan of a modern house with the features that he wanted. The house would be a split-level, which was a popular design of the time, with two storeys, but an off-set floor on one side between the upper and lower levels. It would have three bedrooms upstairs, two bathrooms, a living/dining room as well as a kitchen, a den, a spacious basement with a fruit cellar, and a garage.

Jim worked on many of the simpler tasks himself such as some carpentry and bricklaying, then hired friends or other contractors to complete the rest. His Dutch pals John Van Grootel did much of the carpentry, George Westerdyk fitted in the plumbing and Paul Ten Westeneind installed the electrical wiring. The approximate cost for building such a fine house was about $6000. The Ontario government provided a grant for building a new house so that helped.

Jim was laying the house foundation on November 22, 1963, the day that US President John F. Kennedy was assassinated. The news of that tragic event was such a milestone moment in history that many would remember where they were at the moment for the rest of their lives. With steady work over winter, the house took shape, first the overall form of walls, bricks, and roof on the outside, then installing the drywall, plaster, and flooring on the inside. The split-level home was completed by winter's end. The young family moved into the sparkling new domicile in the spring of 1964.

There would be a change in Jim's working life, too. He returned to work for Rundle Garden Centre after the demise of Oshawa Home

*The split-level house that Jim built on Townline Road
photo taken after an ice storm.*

Landscaping, but in a different capacity. He maintained a strong relationship with Albert and in some ways the balding man with his white moustache was like a father figure. The garden centre really needed to rejuvenate the landscaping sector and Albert felt sure that Jim had what it took. He was offered a full partnership in the business for the handsome fee of $5000.

Rundle's was then the largest garden centre in Oshawa, a good place to be as the city was growing with continual construction of new houses that needed trees, lawns, and gardens. With Jim on board, Rundle Garden Centre became a four-way partnership, between Albert, his daughter Lynda, and Bill Human. Jim took full charge of the landscape contracting component of the business. He went out on job sites with a crew of labourers, doing a lot of the physical planting, sod laying and setting out rock gardens. He also made visits to customers in the evenings to drum up more business just as he had with OHL. Lynda was responsible for maintaining the bookkeeping and managing the garden centre. Good natured Bill maintained and ordered inventory and played a large management role as well. Albert was the face of the business; he could almost always be found on the premises.

In addition to selling plants and gardening supplies, Rundle's sold lawn mowers, rototillers, and chainsaws. They had a small engine repair shop run by Albert's brother Ken who was not an invested partner. Ken serviced machines with a special talent for bringing a dead motor back to life. Yard maintenance, snow removal, a gift shop and Christmas tree sales rounded out the activities that the garden centre was engaged in.

Rundle was the first garden centre established in the Oshawa area, and one of the first in the province of Ontario. Albert originally purchased the 1-acre property at 1015 King Street East in 1945, then on the city outskirts. He started a small landscaping business, first running it alone, but then hired a few helpers as his workload increased. He planted and grew small trees and other nursery stock on the property to use on his planting jobs since there were so few suppliers. Then he developed a small shop that sold box plants, trees, shrubs, and various other items for the yard that eventually developed into a full-fledged garden centre. Albert also purchased a rough piece of hilly land near Castleton where he planted and pruned thousands of pine and spruce that would later be sold as Christmas trees.

Verna, his wife and business partner, ran the office and store, while Albert and a small crew worked on the yards of his growing list of the residential customers. They worked as a team and the operation

Albert Rundle at Rundle Garden Centre about 1961.

continued to expand. Without warning, Verna suddenly died from heart failure in late 1960. Albert was at a complete loss. Distraught and disheartened, he lost the zeal for landscaping and couldn't bring himself to continue with the mental and physical demands involved with it. He was now a single parent with three daughters to raise and support. He continued operating the garden centre but phased out landscaping. The eldest daughter Lynda had different career plans but that was about to change. She was catapulted into the family business with the loss of her mother. Jim was brought on to resurrect the landscaping component, an essential complement to the garden centre.

Business improved for Rundle Garden Centre. Before long Jim's drive, organization, and hard work made landscaping the most profitable sector of the company. Albert's family moved out and the Kamstra family moved into the two-storey home immediately beside the garden center at 1015 King Street in early 1966. That way Jim could be right on the premises of the business, keeping a watchful eye. Not certain where the future would go, Jim decided to retain ownership of the house that he built on Townline Road. It was deliberately rented out to a devout Seventh Day Adventist family who did not smoke or drink. Jim felt assured that these good people would not abuse his investment.

The Rundle house was only about a kilometre from St. Gertrude's Catholic School where the boys attended. They could now walk from home without having to take the city bus. Jamie felt that his name no longer suited him so he proclaimed to the family and others that from now on he would be "James." Theodore had a similar revelation and asked that everyone call him "Ted". Corry carted off James, Harry, and Ted to church services at St. Gertrude's each Sunday morning. Jim rarely made a showing except for midnight mass on Christmas eve. Those were special services with the singing of Christmas carols, and only once a year so Jim was good with that. Attending midnight mass became a family tradition, followed by everyone opening their presents.

Jim and the other partners at Rundle Garden Centre formed the Oshawa Chapter of the Ontario Nursery Trades Association along with the owners of several other landscape related businesses. This mixed group that included greenhouses, landscapers, tree retailers and sod growers met regularly to discuss items of common interest such as distribution, new regulations and promotion.

Members of the Oshawa Chapter of Ontario NurseryTrades Association in 1965 including all four partners of Rundle Garden Centre. Back row: Henk Kobes, Gerry Hazek, Harry Van Belle, Ian Smith, Jim Kamstra, Albert Rundle. Front row: Martin Versluis, Lynda Rundle, Bill Human.

Meanwhile, in the Netherlands, Corry's father, Jan, died on June 4, 1965, from a heart attack. It was unexpected as he was only 64. Corry flew over briefly to attend the funeral. Her youngest sister, Ria, was tasked with taking care of her ailing mother, Cecilia, suffering from the downward spiral of Alzheimer's Disease. The task became more and more demanding as the dementia progressed. It was no way for a vibrant 20-year-old woman to spend her youth. When she was no longer manageable the family put Cecilia into a facility that could handle dementia patients. She died on August 25, 1968.

After years of such daughterly devotion, Ria needed a break, she was ready to begin her own life. Corry encouraged her to come to Canada, where three of her sisters already resided. With such an invitation she did not take long to make a decision. She packed what she needed, leaving most of her belongings behind then emigrated in

May 1966. She flew across the ocean in six hours, unlike her sisters who came by boat, taking at least six days.

Then 23 years of age, she moved in with Jim, Corry and the family, into an upstairs bedroom. Ria, kind and easy-going, was instantly a part of the family, almost like a big sister to the boys and a real help around the house for Corry. She soon was able to find employment at Coles Bookstore in the Oshawa Shopping Centre.

Unfortunately, Jim's contentment at Rundle Garden Centre was short-lived. The profits were being split between four partners and there was not really enough for all of them to make a good living. Albert was well known in the community and a sociable chap so he could drum up business, but his hard-working days were in the past. Bill was suffering from multiple sclerosis so his ability to work was limited. Jim was also at times, frustrated with Lynda who purchased great amounts of giftware and other items that often did not sell well. The partnership was no longer working for him. It was time to get out.

A business partnership requires collaboration, compromise and trust. Because of his drive and need for independence, maybe the concept of sharing the reigns would never work. Jim wanted and needed to be in control. Next time he would go it alone and be able to call all the shots. If things messed up it would be his responsibility. He could deal with that. Jim gave his resignation and divested his shares from the company. Disappointment must have shown in Albert's eyes the day that Jim broke the news.

Rundle Garden Centre continued without Kamstra, but it was not the same, and would soon undergo more changes. A new partner, Stan Konarowski, was brought in to replace Jim. Lynda sold out her shares and left in 1973. Albert stayed on another year or two, but then he was ready for retirement. He had built up and operated that business for over three decades, that was good enough for him. Stan ran the shop for several years before selling it to Herb and Nellie Lamers in 1979. The Lamers' ran the company under the good "Rundle Garden Centre" name at the same location until 2010, when they closed the business for good. After that the old buildings stood vacant for another ten years before being torn down for a new development.

CHAPTER 11

Striking Out with his Own Business

Jim formed a new company which he called "J. Kamstra Landscaping."

"If you have a good name, you should stand behind it," Jim proclaimed to his sons. "People will remember you better than if you give your business some run of the mill name."

The family moved back to the house that Jim built on Townline Road in early 1967. The tea-totalling tenants had left the building in fine shape except that their dog had torn up part of the carpet on the stairs so that needed replacement. The boys were back riding the Oshawa city bus as a means of getting back and forth to school. A year later, however, a new school, called Pope John XXIII, opened within walking distance.

Months before the move, while at one of the monthly Dutch Club dances, Corry introduced Ria to Tony Stolk, a tall, dark-haired outspoken Dutchman. Dapper and smooth-talking, Tony charmed his way into the heart of the blonde Huitenga. They dated for several months before he asked for her hand in marriage.

Tony also had much in common with Jim. They shared an entrepreneurial spirit, an opinionated outlook, both were highly critical of government, and had a love for socializing and singing Dutch songs. The two would become lifelong friends. Ria and Tony made their vows on June 17, 1967 at St. Gertrude's church. Jim acted in the role as father of the bride, and led Ria in white, down the aisle to the grinning groom.

Jim and Corry offered their home for the wedding reception later in the day. Friends and relatives packed into the living room and food was catered in. The warm, sunny June afternoon turned dark. Thunder and lightning followed by a torrential downpour kept all of the guests stuck inside. The capacity of their rural dug well was not sufficient for that many people washing hands and flushing toilets. The taps refused to spit out any more water halfway through the dinner. The party went on, nonetheless. The ladies had to contend with stinky toilets while the men stepped outside to relieve themselves in the backyard. The water table rebounded to refill the well next day.

Jim leading Ria down the church aisle at her wedding.

The Townline property became the base of the new company. It included a vacant lot on the north side of the house where Jim erected a semi-circular Quonset hut of corrugated galvanized steel, known as a Wonder Barn. He needed to purchase the right equipment for the business which included a tractor, a dump truck, a pickup, and a stake truck, as well as lawnmowers, chainsaws and various hand tools. He could park two vehicles and store all the tools and maintenance equipment in the Quonset hut. A den on the lower floor of the split-level house would be the office.

Corry became the bookkeeper, looking after invoicing and the employees' payroll, just as she had done for Oshawa Home Landscaping. She enrolled in a night course to upgrade her skills. Jim planted several rows of tree and shrub seedlings in whatever vacant land remained behind the Quonset hut. Anything that he could grow himself instead of purchase would cut costs and increase revenue. Any space left on the half-acre property was used to store some landscaping materials such as topsoil and rockery stone. He followed the Dutch approach to efficient land use.

Harry learning about gardening at a young age, hoeing the garden at the Townline property in 1967.

The next item on the list was human resources: Jim needed employees who could do much of the labour. He hired a few acquaintances that he met through Rundle Garden Centre. Rene Bassie, a fellow Dutchman who would look after yard maintenance, was the first employee. Next on the payroll was John te Boekhorst, another conscientious Dutchman who would be foreman of a sodding and planting crew. John had previously owned a small landscaping firm himself, so he came with a wide range of practical experience. Since that business went sour, John had no more interest in running his own show. Jim also coerced Morley Travis to join him, a local lad that he had hired at age 21, while at Rundles.

Morley bore a striking resemblance to country singer Jerry Reed with his curly blonde locks, dimpled chin and muscular slim build. As he was the tenth child of seventeen, Morley did not have much opportunity for higher education, but he worked hard and had a particular affinity for machinery. He could operate a tractor with remarkable dexterity, manipulating the bucket to dig earth or move material as if it was part of his body. Morley had an easy-going way about him. He would laugh at his own jokes and would do pretty much whatever was asked without question. Jim recognized his mechanical savvy and loyalty. Ultimately Morley would work for Kamstra longer than anybody else.

Others would be hired as needed. Many were European immigrants, and there were men from the Maritime provinces, who arrived because work continued to be scarce there. Jim could relate to those fellows from his days in Nova Scotia. In the first few years of the business, he would need to have about eight employees through the growing season, as long as the ground was unfrozen. Winter was always a slow time in the business. With the sale of the last Christmas tree in December, the garden centre closed until April. Most employees were also off for the winter, but Jim secured snow removal contracts and kept a few men on the payroll, usually just Morley, John and Rene.

Thus, over the years, Jim saw hundreds of employees. Some stayed with Kamstra Landscaping for decades, and some only lasted a day. Jim recognized the value of employees. To make some real money, he needed able workers that would do much of the physical labour, freeing him to find more contracts yet finding reliable workers was a challenge.

Landscape labourers do not require much education, so he hired people from many walks of life. Applicants received a quick interview where Jim would try to assess their willingness to work more than anything else, but also consider their experience. He would hire them on the spot or turn them down. Once on the job, Jim would closely watch how they worked. They could be planting trees, cutting grass, setting patios, driving trucks or operating a front-end loader. Did they catch on quickly, or did they stand on the side, waiting to be told what to do? Many did not pass Jim's scrutiny and were soon looking elsewhere for work. Many others did, however. They liked the outdoor physical work and the variety of tasks at different job sites. Jim was a fair boss, but his expectations were high, and he had no patience for lacklustre labourers.

Many employees only viewed landscape labourer as a temporary vocation. It was hard physical work that needed to be done outside in all kinds of weather. Then they would be laid off in the winter. There were few benefits and little job security. Several bright young employees greatly pleased Jim as they proved to be effective and efficient workers. However, these men treated their working days at Kamstra Landscaping as a learning ground, to gain experience. They would work for one season then the following year, start up their own fledgling landscape operations and become a competitor. Jim could not blame them, for he had done the same. Nevertheless, it frustrated him.

Thinking about them years later, Jim fondly remembered some of the people he hired, in particular some seasonal migrant workers from Portugal. They would spend the seven warm months in Canada to work then return home to their families in the winter. These were hard workers; they learned fast and were willing to toil for long days on just about any kind of task. They had names like Armando, Antonio, Victor, Salvador, Jose, and Phillip. At one point, however, some of the Portuguese crew talked among each other and concluded that they were underpaid. Together they approached Jim and demanded a $2 per hour raise or they would find work elsewhere. Jim did not give it to them; maybe he thought they were bluffing but they weren't, and they did quit. Soon after they left, Jim realized he had made an error.

Jim visited two of his former hard-working employees in their homeland of Portugal in 1976. Salvador Ganhao on the left and Jose on the right.

The labour that he derived from such efficient employees was worth what they were asking for. He regretted not giving in a little, but it was done, and they were gone.

Winter work was less hectic for the few employees that remained... most of the time. Snow removal was a tricky business because snow would come down when it pleased. There was no telling when the men would be needed. Jim closely monitored weather reports to know when the next snowfall was forecast. Best to wait for the falling snow to stop or driveways would have to be plowed twice. Often, they had to work all through the night to be able to clean parking lots empty of cars and avoid traffic on the roads. Jim installed plows on the front of the four-wheel drive pickup trucks, and he did much of the work himself. Sometimes his sons would come along to shovel off sidewalks and laydown salt on steps.

On these winter forays, Jim frequently encountered vehicles stuck in a snowy ditch. If he saw stranded people present, poorly dressed and clearly in need, he would stop, roll down the window and call out. "Need some help?"

"Why, yes please" was the usual reply.

He would attach a chain between his pickup and the vehicle, pull it out, disconnect the chain, then be on his way. He never asked for payment; he just wanted to help someone in need when he had the power to do so. Nevertheless, a banknote often was thrust in his face as thanks.

Pietje, Jim's mother, visited Canada in September 1969. She was 67 and wanted to see her two sons and their adopted homeland. She boarded an international airliner for the first time in her life. Bauke did not come this time but would visit a few years later. She doted on the grandchildren that she barely knew and could barely communicate with.

Pietje's brother Peter, who had immigrated to California in the 1930s, had never been back to visit the old country. Since Pietje had not seen him in over forty years, Jim picked up the phone and called to invite Peter over. Peter drove his little pickup truck with a camper on the back, accompanied by a small dog, across the continent. The meeting between Peter and Pietje was emotional but awkward. Pietje spoke almost no English, and Peter, away from Holland for so long, remembered very little Dutch. Nevertheless, the way they first looked at each other, and from the tears that flowed, it was clear that there was still much love between them.

CHAPTER 12

Moving it All to Taunton

Jim was not always attentive to laws and regulations, and he did not always investigate to see if rules even applied. One day Darlington Township notified him that J. Kamstra Landscaping was running a business on property that did not conform to the land use zoning, in addition to unlawful storage of materials. Jim ignored the first letter but was issued a summons and knew that he could only evade that issue for so long. He hired a lawyer with the firm McNeely and Marks to assist in the civil lawsuit. The presentation made by Jim and his lawyer resulted in a successful plea. The case was dropped without charge.

Nevertheless, the Townline property was getting too small to run the business anyway. It was situated in a residential area at the edge of the expanding city. The lot would soon be crammed in among shops and houses. Certainly, there was no place to expand there. Jim looked for a larger tract further out of the city. A friend and acquaintance who was also a real estate magnate, J.J. Van Herwaarden, alerted Jim to a parcel on Taunton Road that showed promise. It was only about five kilometres north of the current operation with frontage on a busy road, which meant good visibility to potential customers. At 8 hectares (20 acres), it was a huge tract of land compared to what he had. The asking price was $25,000, a small fortune that he really could not afford. There was an option to purchase half of the parcel for half of the cost, an easier 'pill to swallow'.

"Buy the whole damn thing," J.J. strongly advised. "You can't go wrong."

J.J. was a sophisticated gentleman, well-educated and a shrewd businessman with interests in several companies. Jim respected his opinion. He purchased the land outright in 1968 and acknowledged years later how right the older man had been.

The property sloped gently downward from east to west. It was well-drained with fertile stony soil. There were two tenanted houses, both in poor shape, as well as a large wooden barn that had once been used for cattle and still stored hay in the loft. A few years before, the land had been an operating farm of crops and pasture but was now fallow, consisting mostly of open fields with a few hedgerows separating them and a laneway leading to the back. The Quonset building at Townline was dismantled, moved and reassembled. Jim demolished one of the houses, while one of his workers, Gerrit Burtenum, rented the other.

Gerrit was a quiet balding Dutchman, with white hair on the fringes. He could barely speak English and was perhaps the most loyal employee Jim ever had. Jim allowed Gerrit to live there on easy rent. The barn was cleaned up, structurally reinforced, and the wooden floor repaired to enable the storage of equipment both upstairs and down.

In addition to landscaping, Jim decided to open a garden centre on the spacious site. An architect developed a functional two-phase plan for the office and store. An office, a washroom, and a small store were constructed first. The second phase entailed an expanded store to be constructed at a later date. They planted many rows of small trees on the southern half of the property, creating an extensive tree nursery. A shade house and a plastic covered greenhouse were erected for growing and displaying smaller plants. Tractor-trailers arrived at the yard unloading skids of fertilizer, patio slabs, rockery stone and peat moss. Early spring of 1970, the garden centre opened its doors to the public, fully stocked and ready for customers.

The Kamstra family needed to move to the site as well, but the shabby little house where Gerrit now resided would not do. A brand-new house would be built on the premises, handy to the shop and garden centre. Jim and Corry looked over various designs to come up with a home that would fit their needs, then hired an architect to draft up a blueprint. No more "split-level.'" This would be a modern house with a carport, fireplace, built-in vacuum system, fruit cellar, and carpeted floors. As with the previous house, Jim subcontracted the construction but used his employees to do as much of the grunt work as much as possible.

The Townline property was listed on the real estate market and sold sooner than anticipated. The Kamstra family had to move out at the end of August. Problem was the new house was not even

Announcing

MR. JAMES KAMSTRA'S

OPENING OF . . .

J. KAMSTRA

LANDSCAPING & GARDEN MAINTENANCE COMPANY

Mr. Kamstra now opening his own business comes from Rundle Garden Centre, where he served as vice-president and later as president of that company. Now Mr. Kamstra, president of J. KAMSTRA COMPANY offers you his 12 years knowledge and experience in the landscaping and garden maintenance field. Try us you'll be glad you did.

MR. JAMES KAMSTRA

ORDER NOW! YOUR EARLY SPRING FERTILIZING
And be the first on your street with a beautiful green lawn
—also Order Now Your . . .

Ad that Jim placed in the Oshawa Times announcing the opening of the garden centre in Spring 1970.

started yet. But yes, there was that rustic two-bedroom bungalow, still better than where Jim and Corry lived in the first days of their marriage. Gerrit and his wife moved out, and the Kamstras moved into this temporary home that they affectionately called "the shack."

Work on the new house proceeded immediately and expediently through the autumn. An excavator dug out an enormous hole just behind the shack where the basement would be. John Van Grootel laid concrete blocks on the foundation, helped by his sons Andy and Ronald. He also framed the floor joists and walls. Garitano's churning cement trucks came in to pour the concrete slurry into the basement that would form the floor. The concrete had to set, but once achieving the desired consistency, workers had limited time to smooth it out before it firmed up. The tradesmen worked their trowels late into the night. There were also plasterers, bricklayers, plumbers, electricians, roofers, carpet installers, and more. Pierre, a French stonemason, artistically fitted pieces of fieldstone to the front giving the L-shaped bungalow a distinctive appearance from the roadside. In three and a half months, the beautiful brick house was complete. The Kamstras moved in just before Christmas.

Appliances and everything thing else were moved the 30 metres from of the shack to the new house. The forlorn shack sat empty only a few days. Jim loaded live shells into the barrel of his 303 Dutch army rifle. He handed the gun to all three boys, letting them have a turn firing through the ceiling from the inside. The gun bucked with each shot, feeling like a kick to their shoulders. Then he tied a heavy chain around a corner of the injured house and pulled it down to the ground with a tractor. In only one day, the beloved shack was rendered into rubble.

One of the critical considerations for running a successful business can be summed up in the well-known saying: "location, location, location." In this regard, Jim had chosen wisely. Traffic constantly flowed along Taunton Road since it was a major thoroughfare heading east out of Oshawa. The new garden centre could not be missed by anyone driving by. Jim hung up huge wooden letters spelling "Kamstra Landscaping" on the side of the white-walled office so that passers-by would know the name. A little out of town, but there weren't many other garden centres in the area. Besides, urban-dwelling customers enjoyed getting out into the country to see and buy the flowers and shrubs that they could plant in their gardens.

The garden centre bustled from April to June when winter-weary customers were eager to plant gardens and shape up their yards before the lazy days of summer. The planting season is short, and customers did most of their gardening on weekends. Consequently, the garden centre had to stay open all day Saturday, but Sunday as well. Sunday shopping was a novel concept in the early 1970s. Jim and Corry worked seven days a week through April, May, and June. Much of Corry's time was spent behind the counter, selling plants, and garden supplies. She was also responsible for billing and bookkeeping, which became ever more complicated with more employees, more stock, and changing tax laws. It was getting to be too much for her, and each year would be busier than the year before.

Kamstra hired additional help to work the store and with the books. Elaine Shewring and later her sister, Vivian Carrette, took over much of the book work. As the pace of business intensified, Jim re-

Aerial view of Kamstra Landscaping property in 1972 showing office/store, greenhouse, storage barn and house where the Kamstras resided.

alized that they should hire a manager to run the garden centre. He first tried Myra Granger, who grew and sold plants from her greenhouse for years. She was an expert at growing plants and friendly with customers but not the most diligent at keeping the garden centre organized. A few years later, Dorothy Shade managed the garden centre effectively, assisted by Karen Iliffe. Kamstra also hired Dorothy's burly, truck-driving husband Wayne to make deliveries of soil and nursery stock. The pace eventually became too much. After a couple of years, Dorothy gave her resignation then moved away with her husband to a slower-paced part of the province.

    A promising candidate named Ron White applied as manager. His credentials were impressive. He had operated a large centre for White Rose, a giant garden retailer in Toronto. Ron was a good organizer as long as he had underlings who could do most of the labour. Running a small garden centre like Kamstra's demanded multitasking and physical work, which was too much for him. Ron did not last long. Managing the garden centre required high organizational skills, motivation, and extended hours during the spring rush. Only the most dedicated employee would be willing to put in the work and live up to Jim's demanding expectations.

Jim wanted to focus more of his attentions on landscaping since it proved to be more lucrative than the retail sales in the garden centre. Jim could secure large contracts with home builders who were constructing entire subdivisions around the ever-growing City of Oshawa. Some of his major clients included Armstrong Homes, Halminen Homes, Jeffrey Homes, and Marianna Developments. Grading, sodding, tree planting, and laying patios for dozens of houses in one swoop would keep a couple of crews busy for weeks. One of the most significant projects he ever won was Wilmot Creek Retirement Community in Newcastle for Rice Construction. Hundreds of houses, as well as a golf course and a community centre, were constructed on this 50-hectare parcel, all planted by Kamstra Landscaping over several years in the late 1970s.

Jim did his best to ensure that every aspect of the business ran smoothly, but there were so many moving parts. He knew that the most essential element of running any business was getting paid. One of the disadvantages of large landscape contracts was that the work usually had to be completed and inspected before the client would pay their invoice. Kamstra Landscaping often had invested thousands of dollars in plant materials and labour in a job before any money was received. Delayed payments created problems with cash flow, but much worse were clients who did not pay at all.

Jim did not let those outstanding invoices slip his attention. When one was months overdue, Jim would go into action. He would call the client daily, harassing the secretary if the boss was unreachable. He showed up at their office or even their home, if necessary, to collect an overdue cheque. It didn't always work, and sometimes he resorted to legal action, which also did not always work. If a company declared bankruptcy, they were legally discharged from their financial obligations. Jim would have no recourse to collect, or even to reclaim his materials. Some unscrupulous business owners had a reputation for declaring bankruptcy, getting out of their debts, then starting up a new debt-free company under a different company name.

Jim should have known better when a particular Dutch builder contracted Kamstra Landscaping to lay sod and install plant material around a series of houses under construction. Kamstra completed the job on schedule, and the client appeared to be satisfied. Soon after that, however, Jim received notification that the company had declared bankruptcy before making any payments.

Jim exploded. "That bastard, stiffing me like this!"

With a couple of his most trusted employees, and under cover of darkness, Jim drove out to the unoccupied houses with a flatbed truck. Quickly and quietly as possible, they dug up all of the trees and shrubs that they had planted earlier. The nursery stock was not brought back to the main yard however, but hauled to Kamstra's other property, where it was planted in among an existing plantation.

The next day the Dutch builder saw the empty holes in his subdivision and thought he could smell a rat. He felt pretty sure that Jim had come to retrieve the plants in the night. These were no longer Kamstra's property according to the law. He reported the stolen plants to the police, telling them that the thief was probably Jim Kamstra. A constable in uniform appeared at the garden centre, asking to see Jim. With a straight face, Jim denied knowing anything about the event.

"Mind if I take a look around the premises?" asked the man in blue.

"Sure, go right ahead."

The constable took a walk among the rows of trees, found nothing suspicious and soon left.

CHAPTER 13

Leisure Time and Family Vacations

One of Jim's philosophies was work hard, play hard. Although many would have called him a workaholic, Jim was not the kind of obsessive business owner who felt that running the shop was so important that he could not take a vacation once in a while. He loved his time off, but when he took it, he made sure not to waste it.

In the 1960s, Jim and Corry regularly took their kids out for a drive or excursion on Sundays throughout the year. Sometimes there was a dual purpose. Jim would investigate a property he was interested in, or to check out Christmas tree plantations to see if the trees were worthy of cutting and selling later in December. Often these were walks along country road allowances, along creeks or woodlands, interesting spots that he either knew or just wanted to investigate. Whether the land was a public park or private property didn't seem to matter.

On one spring outing, he drove along a rutted track through a cow pasture. The family car splashed into a deep puddle with a soft bottom, sinking up to its axles in mud. It was good and stuck. Jim knew what to do. He pulled the jack out of the trunk, jacked up the vehicle and placed cedar fence rails under the tires. The farmer was none too pleased to see a vehicle along with a family in his pasture, however. He charged Jim with trespassing. After some back-and-forth bantering, Jim pulled out his wallet and handed the farmer a few bills. At least that got the old man off of his back.

Jim bought a heavy canvas tent in the early 1960s to use for family vacations since it would provide an inexpensive means to get a taste of the great outdoors. Ontario was endowed with many scenic places where one could camp. At a provincial park near Ottawa, Jim, Corry, and Ted had their sleeping bags set out in the big canvas while James and Harry slept in their own pint-sized pup tent. The boys turned in early while the parents stayed up for a nightcap at the crackling campfire. Before turning in, they looked in on the pup tent.

James lay asleep in his bag, but where was little Harry? He was not inside. They shone a flashlight around and caught sight of a lumpy sleeping bag at the bottom of a slope. Harry was in it, still asleep, but how did he get down there? He must have rolled out of the open tent, and down the hill still wrapped within his bag.

More worrying, Harry was not alone. A curious pair of skunks were sniffing around the sleeping boy. The nosy little animals seemed harmless enough. The parents watched from a distance, wary of making a sudden move that could make the mustelids unleash their notorious spray. After a few minutes, they wandered off into the forest, searching for something more interesting.

Camping was exciting for the boys and their dad but not so great for mom. She wasn't an outdoor person to start with, and camping meant organizing the kids' clothing, preparing meals on a Coleman stove, hauling water, smelly outhouses, and sleeping in a tent on uneven ground. When rain fell, it was even worse, with wet sleeping bags and grumpy boys. Not much fun, just more work without the conveniences! Meanwhile, the boys were enjoying themselves, fishing and exploring. After a few summer adventures, Jim and Corry gave up on family car camping.

Still, Jim appreciated nature and shared what lore he knew with the boys. He could make a whistle from a willow twig; he knew all about trees and the names of common birds. These Sunday outings had a greater influence on James than on Harry or Ted, for he really would develop a passion for exploring nature and the great outdoors. On one outing, Jim sighted a crow flying off a jumble of sticks high in a tree. Jim climbed up to the nest, spotted four greenish speckled eggs that he took out and carefully placed in a can with tissue paper. Later at home, he showed James how to prick holes at both ends, then blow out the yolk and albumen, leaving a hollow perfectly preserved egg.

"When I was a boy, I had an egg collection. Maybe you would like to start one too?"

That was the start of James' lifelong birding pursuits. Jim was intent on obtaining a young crow that they could raise as a pet, just as he had done when he was a boy. Acquiring one meant first finding an active crow nest containing young. It became a springtime quest for father and son. While driving between job sites during the week, Jim might spot a pair of crows at a woodlot that seemed to be a likely nest location. The following Sunday, Jim and James would wake up while the rest of the family slept, then head out to the promising woodlot. They walked through cedar dominated valleys checking tree by tree for a sign of a nest. When a nest was spotted, Jim would send up James, who become an adept climber in the process.

If the nest was in a pine with sturdy spaced branches, the climb was easy. Sometimes the nest was high above the ground in a spindly cedar lacking any branches below four metres. James stood on Jim's shoulders, reached up to grab tightly on the trunk with both hands, then hopped onto the tree. Jim placed a pole under James' foot and pushed the boy up until James could reach the first branch to be able to pull himself up. The lowest branches were always dead and scarcely able to hold his weight. James pressed his feet tight at the base, praying that the limb did not snap off. Up he climbed until his head rose above the nest to be able to look in. Usually, he would find just an empty depression, so he would ease his way back down and carry on searching for another nest.

Jim with Willy the pet crow being fed by James. Ted and Harry are sitting in between.

The father and son team carried on the crow hunt for several springs. Their success rate was low, but both relished those Sunday morning outings. Success came at last in May 1969. James made an easy climb up a wide branching crack willow to a nest containing four black feathered nestlings with mouths agape but a bit too young to remove from their parents. They returned in a week to steal one young out of the nest.

James named the bird Willy for the type of tree it was found. The noisy bird was so easy to feed, it ravenously gulped down canned dog food.

"Caw, caw, caw, glug glug glug," Willy said.

Willy proved to be a most intelligent pet and a fine companion for the boy that summer. In the mornings, it flew up to the window of his second storey window, pecking at the pane until James let it in. Sometimes the silly bird would sit on James' shoulder as he rode his bike. Then one day, Willy just disappeared. Did he fly off to join other crows, or did someone steal him? James never saw his beloved black friend again.

For his twelfth birthday, Harry asked for a dog. That is all he wanted, nothing else.

"I will get you a dog under one condition," Jim promised. "You have to look after it; that means feeding and cleaning up after it."

They went to the Oshawa Dog Pound to see what they could find. A black Labrador Retriever puppy sat in one pen, wagging its tail and staring up at Harry. That was the one. Harry was so thrilled. Although a female, Hector would be her name. Jim rigged up a steel pen with a doghouse in the backyard where it would stay overnight. Harry played with Hector endlessly during the day and fed it obediently in the evenings.

After several days, dog feces began accumulating in the pen.

"Time to clean up the poop," Jim advised.

A few days later, it still hadn't been cleaned.

"Harry, clean out the pen!" Jim ordered sternly. "Or no supper for you."

"No, it's gross, it stinks!" he cried.

"Well, no supper until you do it!"

Harry could be stubborn, and today he was. He just walked away, straight to the back of the property, then across the farm fields beyond. Corry was concerned. From the kitchen window, she could see the form of Harry getting smaller and smaller in the distance until he was a mere dot. How far would he go? Should they go and get him? Then she looked at the dot. Was it getting bigger? Yes, it was, Harry was coming back. Without a word, Harry grabbed a shovel to scoop the poop out of Hector's pen. Then he went in for supper.

Harry washing his dog Hector after she was sprayed by a skunk.

Summer holidays from school lasted ten weeks for the boys. Jim, however, had a business to run so usually could afford no more than one precious week for the annual family vacation. In July 1970, the family made a seven-hour drive north to Cochrane in to catch the Polar Bear Express for Moosonee. It was their first time travelling this far into northern Ontario to visit a rather isolated First Nation community. Jim led the family through the rutted dirt roads of the village. Ever curious about people and their economy, Jim freely approached a Native family standing outside of their tarpaper and plastic covered shack, to enquire about what life was like here. Instead of expressing annoyance at a nosy stranger, the stocky father willingly told Jim about frigid winters, trapping to supplement his income and the community's isolation.

The family learned something about Canada's first peoples through their visit north. Meanwhile central Ontario is well-known as a land of lakes. Spending sunny days on the dockside at a cottage remains a popular way for the middle class to enjoy their free time in summer. Many of Jim's friends and acquaintances were cottage owners, and some would freely lend theirs to him for a family vacation. Albert Rundle gave use of his rustic cottage on Foote's Lake near Huntsville for a week in 1965 and 66. Paul Ten Westeneind owned a more distant cottage on a rocky islet in the middle of Lake Temagami that the Kamstras could use. Close friends Ulrich and Edith Strahl made their Kasshabog Lake cottage available in 1971 and 1972. Swimming, fishing, boating, water skiing, playing badminton, and exploratory excursions were all part of the fun.

Jim was content to borrow someone's cottage on occasion but did not feel the need to own one himself. However, while on a Sunday drive in October 1972, a "cottage for sale" sign along the Trent River caught his eye. He decided to look into real estate listings, then said to his wife, "This is a good deal, a good investment. Let's buy it."
Corry liked it, too (*way better than camping*, she thought) so the Kamstras became proud cottage owners.

The wooden cottage was a complete package, fully furnished, and even came with a separate guest house. The well treed lot was comfortably huddled in among a handful of other cottages and faced an undeveloped forested shoreline on the opposite side of the river. Furthermore, it was an easy commute for weekend getaways being only a ninety-minute drive from home. They used their little piece of paradise to entertain friends. They also generously lent it out to visiting Dutch relatives and friends, payback for the cottages that they had borrowed. Fishing was quite good in the wide river, with pickerel, bass, and pike to keep Jim occupied.

The cottage had a few drawbacks, though. The offshore water was weedy and somewhat turbid, not the most pleasant for swimming. Also, the main channel of the Trent Canal extended just offshore. Summer saw heavy traffic from houseboats and pleasure craft. The family would stay at the cottage for one week in summer, on long weekends, and occasionally in the winter with snowmobiles.

After a while, however, Jim concluded that he was not a cottage-committed person, not the type to join the mass exodus every weekend for their piece of lakefront or to spend their holidays at the same place year after year. It was also another property that required maintenance. Jim sold the Trent River real estate for a healthy profit in the autumn of 1975 after owning it for just three years. He would never buy another.

The Kamstras soon developed a taste for more exotic destinations. Their first foreign vacation was very short. Jim took Corry to Bermuda to commemorate their tenth wedding anniversary. Originally, the trip was booked for September 1966, but a hurricane headed for the island on the scheduled date, forcing them to rebook it for November. It was just the two them at a subtropical resort without the kids; it was like a second honeymoon.

When the boys were a little older, the parents felt that it was time they experience and appreciate the land of their heritage. The family boarded a KLM airliner for a three-week trip to the Netherlands in March 1971. James, Harry, and Ted were taken out of school knowing that such a trip would provide a better education. They were reacquainted with their extended family on both sides. Jim's parents had rarely ever seen their grandchildren, so this visit was special for them. Although it wasn't quite the same country as when their Jim and Corry resided there, in many ways it hadn't changed. Meppel and Franeker (Jim and Corry's hometowns) characterized by cobblestone streets, canals and historic gambrel roofed buildings with curving eaves were much the same. The boys learned much about the traumatic World War II period from Jim's boyhood tales and from stagnant military artillery that they viewed and climbed on in an outdoor war museum.

Although far from newlyweds, Jim and Corry had not lost that spark and saw a romantic opportunity. "Let's go to Paris for a few days, just the two of us", Jim suggested. "The boys can stay with relatives."

They boarded a Paris bound jetliner for the one-hour flight. They took in the sites that anyone visiting this famous city must see: the Moulin Rouge, Arc de Triomphe, the Louvre, Notre Dame Cathedral and of course, the Eiffel Tower. They found accommodation in a quaint hotel in the historic section, ate exquisite French cuisine and danced in lively nightclubs. It was like a third honeymoon.

Meanwhile, James boarded with the Wolke family; Corry's sister Suus, her husband Herman and four cousins. Harry and Ted stayed with Jim's parents, Opa Bauke and Oma Pietje. Communication was not easy between them as each knew only a few words of the other's language. Combined with gestures, however, they could understand each other well enough. Pietje, the doting grandmother, spoiled the boys with treats and cooked them delicious meals.

Bauke took Harry, Ted, and their cousin, Jimmy, for an afternoon stroll along the railway tracks. Long dried grasses from the previous year's growth covered the berm along the way. Harry saw his grandfather pull a box of matches from his pocket, strike one, and put it down to the ground. The grasses ignited instantly. In minutes, flames spread along the berm and white smoke began billowing in the air. The boys found it to be more fun than sitting inside. Bauke first smiled, but then grew serious and bellowed out some Dutch orders that Harry and Ted did not understand. He gestured them to follow him under a railway bridge. Harry saw a police car arrive. A pair of officers hurriedly came over to investigate and put out the fire. Luckily the preoccupied policemen did not see the old man and three boys huddled below the bridge, and they eventually left.

Just why did Opa start a fire on public land, especially with children in his care? He just wanted to see it burn. The boys could now understand where their father derived his love of fires; it was a Kamstra thing. The parents returned from France to reclaim their kids for the final leg of their Dutch adventure before returning to Canada.

In March 1973, Jim planned a break from the Ontario winter doldrums. Early on Saturday morning, the family of five took their respective seats in the Buick with bag lunches and packed suitcases for the long drive to Florida. The parents took the kids out of school for the week before March break, giving them sixteen days to play with for an extended, sunny vacation.

The day they left and the preceding few days had been unusually mild for early March. They drove, spending three days cooped up in the southbound car following Interstate 75 to reach St. Petersburg, with hotel stays enroute in Cincinnati and Atlanta. Jim was not keen on Disneyland, the Florida destination for most families, so they bypassed Orlando. They spent half a day on the beach at St. Petersburg, followed by a visit to the famous Busch Gardens.

Jim marvelled at the tropical vegetation, such a variety of exotic plants that can grow and be cultivated. He stopped into a garden centre to compare the operation with his in Ontario. Then everyone back in the car to continue to the south end of the state, Flamingo in the Everglades National Park. There were brief stops to take in a tourist attraction here and there, but most of the time, it was drive, drive, drive.

Between the milder than usual weather when they left Ontario and the summery temperatures in Florida, something started to burn inside Jim. Spring had arrived extra early this year, convincing him that he needed to get home soon and go back to work. Once reaching their southern terminus, the family car changed direction for the long road north. By the time they crossed the Georgia border, the Kamstras had spent only five nights in the Sunshine State. Jim was motoring in the direction of home, like a horse heading back to its barn.

As they continued north, the clear skies turned gray. Snow began falling when they hit the Pennsylvania line and would continue to do so for the rest of the drive home. When they arrived back in Oshawa, mid-winter had returned. It would not be any early spring after all. The boys still had a week off before going back to school.

Almost two years later, Jim received a surprise call from his friend and former business partner, Jack. Janssen revealed that he had been diagnosed with cancer and doctors expected him to live for no more than a year.

"Let's do something old buddy, while we still can. We need to have some fun together, like the old days!".

Along with their wives, they booked a week to an all-inclusive beach resort in Jamaica. Jim offered to take his sons, as well. Heavily into downhill skiing and not keen on hanging out with their parents, Harry and Ted were not interested. James, however, was eager for a trip to the tropics.

The five arrived at the Golden Beach Hotel, east of Ocho Rios, along with a planeload of other winter-weary Canadians. A week of swimming, fishing, drinking, dancing, exploring the island, and occasionally getting swindled by locals, it was memorable for all. In the light-hearted setting and being far removed from their stressful business, James saw his parents in a new light; they had become more like friends than the usual authoritarian figures. Jack and Jim with their boisterous singing, clowning, and lack of inhibition, were perhaps the most conspicuous guests in the Golden Beach Hotel that week. They acted like teenagers, feeding off each other's jokes and antics. The wives and son tried to follow their lead.

Jim and Corry (foreground) with Margaret and Jack Janssen in a fishing boat off the Jamaica coast.

Jim and James dressed as women accompanied by another guest during masquerade party at the Golden Beach Hotel in Jamaica.

Although Jack's condition was never disclosed, a rumour was spreading among the hotel guests that Jack did not have long to live. When someone quietly approached Jim to ask if it was true, he blurted out a little too strongly, "No, it's not true, that's bullshit!"

That probably confirmed for them that it was true.

Shortly after returning to Canada, Jack watched a television program of a highly acclaimed doctor in Germany who was conducting state of the art cancer research and having promising results with new drugs. With nothing to lose, Jack tracked down his number and phoned the doctor immediately to book an appointment. Then, sparing no expense, he booked the first plane he could get for Europe. Jack willingly subjected himself to novel drugs and treatments whose effectiveness was not yet fully proven. His impulsiveness paid off, for Jack was able to enjoy another twelve years of life before finally succumbing to the terrible disease.

In January 1977, when father-son relations had improved from their lowest point, the Kamstra family took a vacation to Nassau in the Bahamas. Although they stayed at an all-inclusive ocean side resort, not a lot of time was spent just lying on the beach soaking up rays. It was just not the Kamstra way. They rented motor scooters and circumnavigated the island over a couple of days. One day Jim rented a runabout with a 20-horsepower outboard motorboat and propelled them across an open stretch of water to an uninhabited island out from New Providence, just to fish and explore.

Even on vacation, Jim could rarely sit still for long.

CHAPTER 14

Paddle Forth

When on the water, Jim usually ventured out in an aluminum rowboat equipped with an outboard motor since that was the ideal fisherman's craft. However, dipping a canoe paddle through glassy waters on an early morning was more in tune with nature and a versatile means of getting around in lake country. Such a sleek craft, tapered to a point at both ends, was so much more efficient than the awkward punts that he rowed as a boy in the Netherlands.

The Kamstra family was introduced to this iconic Canadian form of water travel while they vacationed at the Strahl cottage in August 1971. Once all had mastered the basic technique of paddling, the two available canoes were used extensively. It gave the boys freedom to explore the lake on their own. At other times the parents and kids set out for a day long outing in two canoes, portaging into a picturesque, otherwise inaccessible body of water known as Blind Lake.

Back from their week at the cottage, Jim made a proposition to his three sons. If they all helped out on a landscape job for five days, he would buy the family a brand-new canoe. This they did, and in return, Jim purchased a sleek blue craft which they took for paddles as often as possible. On a sunny September Sunday, Jim suggested a family outing on the Pigeon River. They borrowed a second canoe, then put them in off the side of Highway 115.

Once in the canoes and paddling downstream the world changed within a few bends. The hum of traffic faded into the distance to be replaced by the sound of the ripples. Creek channels often offered long stretches with minimal human evidence since the flood-prone lowlands could not be farmed or built upon. The river started as a channel barely wide enough for a canoe as they penetrated an imposing alder swamp. Branches closed in from both sides and occasional beaver dams blocked their progress. They had to step out, slide the canoe over the dam, then climb back in to continue paddling. The swamp eventually opened into a marsh and the channel widened, torturously meandering towards the lake. At days end, they had only covered half of their expected distance. Jim would not let them stop there! The following weekend the family returned to paddle the rest of Pigeon River to its terminus at Pigeon Lake.

Although he did not become a serious tripper, Jim liked to organize day trips for the family, packing a picnic lunch and choosing a route to follow a nearby river or wide creek. A paddle usually started from a bridge on a roadside. Travelling with the current was the best, the craft would glide through the water with ease as the flowing water did most of the work. Fleetwood Creek, Crowe River, and Percy Reach were among the routes that they had tried.

His most ambitious and adventurous canoe trip was well thought out. Jim and Paul conceived a plan to paddle a 325-kilometre route in Northern Ontario, starting north of Cochrane and ending at Moosonee. In the winter of 1977, they acquired maps and a printed description of the route to plan out the details. Paul chose the route; why they settled on that one is unknown. It was far away, not a regularly travelled canoe route and not even particularly scenic. For such a long trip virtually all the meals would consist of freeze-dried packages to cut down on weight, with the intent of supplementing meals through hunting and fishing.

They put the three fully loaded canoes into the Abitibi River on August 29. Paul's two sons came along: 18-year-old Tony and 14-year-old, Paul Jr. Jim brought his son James (then aged 20), and Bill Loyens from London evened it out as the sixth paddler. They had agreed to leave their watches behind to be free of time obsession. Jim objected but he was overruled. Three canoes set out on the wide turbid Abitibi River making good headway for all were strong paddlers.

On the third day with a brisk wind at their back, Jim had the idea to rig up a sail with a tent fly. The makeshift sail helped propel the single canoe but when they lashed all three together with poles and two tent flies, it worked marvellously; faster, and a lot less tiring than paddling. The wind picked up and the river widened as they entered the reservoir above Abitibi Canyon Dam. Whitecaps formed on the waves; they were really moving now. Tony lost control of the canoe that he was steering, then the canoe ends jammed together. The contraption rotated uncontrollably.

"Get the damn canoes apart or we are going to capsize," Paul yelled.

They very nearly did, but all pushed with paddles to get the canoes apart, then quickly pulled down the sails.

Jim holding up makeshift sail with tent fly on the Abitibi River.

They went ashore to pull the canoes out at the dam. The portage was made easy by a couple of the locals who lived in the small community that housed Ontario Hydro workers that operated the generating station. For a couple shots of whiskey and a few bottles of beer, the workers were happy to haul the canoes and packs over the dam with their pickup truck.

Two days later they reached Otter Rapids, another hydro dam. Below this dam, a canyon with a long treacherous set of turbulent rapids was no match for this group of relatively novice canoeists. Instead, they had to make a three-kilometre portage through the muskeg to reach the Onakawana, a much smaller river that runs parallel with the Abitibi. They would follow it for one hundred meandering kilometres downstream before rejoining the bigger river.

Before the trip, Paul had fabricated a contraption out of a single bicycle wheel that could be strapped to the bottom of the large aluminum canoe to facilitate the rigorous Onakawana portage. With the aluminum canoe full of supplies and with the wheel attached, it took all six of them to balance and push the awkward thing through mudholes and over logs. They unloaded on the bank where they set up camp. Bill found that he had left his tent at the previous campsite. It was too far back. They would just have to double up in the two remaining tents. That made it cozy for Bill was a large man.

Early next morning the three canoes set off down the narrow Onakawana River as it twisted its way through a dense forest of spruce and fir. James and Tony in the first canoe, Bill and Jim in the second, and the two Pauls in the big aluminum canoe at the end. The canoes soon lost sight of each other due to the winding river. A steady current carried them along with many sections of gentle rapids and occasional log jams. Wherever a tree had toppled, it blocked the entire channel, then could trap other logs floating downstream.

The largest log jam acted as a dam creating a natural reservoir with the upstream side about a metre higher than the downstream. James and Tony approached it cautiously, stepped out, lifted the canoe over and got back in to continue paddling. Bill and Jim did the same. When the third canoe came upon the jam, Paul did not observe how far the water dropped on the other side. They sided their canoe to the top log, wobbled, then inadvertently leaned over too far the wrong way. The canoe tipped just far enough that water started spilling over the gunnel. The force of the gushing water rolled the canoe sideways and pushed it hard against the log. They were in trouble.

"Get the stuff out before everything is soaked!" Paul yelled to his son.

They pulled out packs and moved them to the shore. The canoe was now mostly submerged, becoming part of the log jam. The pressure exerted by flowing water held it tightly against the horizontal tree trunks.

The others had no idea of Pauls' predicament. They just moseyed on downstream. Brook trout were plentiful and easy to catch with a baited hook. Bill and Jim were in their element, catching trout after trout until they had a fine string of fifteen pan-sized fish. The two fibreglass crafts stopped and waited for a while, assuming that the aluminum would soon show up. Bill and Tony cleaned fish while Jim built a fire then fried up the fillets in butter. The hungry men soon wolfed down the meal, a delectable treat. With still no sign of the "Pauls", all realized that something must be wrong. James and Tony hopped in their canoe and fought the current to make their way upstream to find out what happened.

Meanwhile, Paul Sr. and Jr. got into the water, pushing and pulling to try to free the silver canoe. It would not budge; the force of flowing water was too strong. With a small hand saw Paul began cutting logs in the jam. He started with the smaller pieces, pulling them out one at a time. Then onto larger logs. It was a tedious task and he worked at it for hours. Paul Jr. set up the tent and built a fire. They might be there overnight, and it gave some shelter from the drizzle. By the time James and Tony found them Paul had removed two-thirds of the logs. Water was gushing through.

"Maybe we can free the canoe with all of us," Paul Sr. suggested.

Paul got into the flowing cold water while James and Tony clambered into the immobile canoe. They grabbed onto the gunnels and with their body weight, rocked the warped craft back and forth. It started to move, slow at first but soon picking up momentum.

"Get out of the way!" yelled Paul.

James hopped out onto the safety of what remained of the log jam, but Tony sat in the bottom of the canoe and could not get out. The force of water sucked the vessel down under the log jam, completely submerging it along with Tony. It kept moving and soon resurfaced beyond the jam about five metres downstream. Tony's head popped up and he gasped for air. He could have been snagged on a submerged log but made it through unscathed.

They pulled the canoe to shore. It was twisted and kinked but still in one piece. Had it been one of the fibreglass canoes, it would have broken into pieces and been unusable. Paul found an aspen log and was able to bang and leverage the hull just enough to make it river worthy. They took down the tent, loaded the canoe, and headed downstream to rejoin Bill and Jim where they set up camp at the lunch spot.

From there it was two full days of paddling down the Onakawana. The flow was steady, and they negotiated their way through countless sets of rapids. They were especially cautious around any further log jams. Since the aluminum canoe was no longer symmetrical, it had become awkward to steer. It did not want to go straight, constantly pulling to one side. The Onakawana emptied its tannin waters into the muddy Abitibi, they were back on big water. Although this trip was not driven by a set schedule, something occurred to Jim. They should try to reach Moosonee by Labour Day, the last day of summer. After that the trains only ran twice a week and they could be stuck there for a few days. With a new sense of urgency, they pushed themselves, paddling steadily for hours on end. When there were rapids that required portaging, they found it was often quicker to line the loaded canoes through with a person on either end, rather than unloading and carrying it all overland.

They arrived at the confluence with the Moose River, a great flowing stretch of water almost two kilometres wide. The final day they all stroked without rest through periods of sun followed by bouts of rain. They rounded a bend and the low white buildings of Moosonee appeared in the distance, still a couple of paddling hours away. They landed onshore with mighty sore arms, finding that the train had left that morning and there would not be another for three days. They should have taken their time.

Bill Loyens, James, Jim, Tony TenWesteneind, Paul Jr. and Paul Sr. TenWesteneind arriving in Moosonee at the end of their 10 day canoe trip.

Disaster can also strike on shorter routes. Jim thought that the Black River might make a pleasant day paddle. In September 1982, Jim took James up for a flight to scout it out. Near the southern edge of the Canadian Shield, the river showed a 14 kilometre wild stretch between roads. Forested banks, clear water, exposed outcrops and occasional rapids but nothing looked too serious. The following weekend, Jim, Corry, James and Harry loaded up the camper with two fibreglass canoes and drove up to Victoria Bridge where they camped for the night.

After next morning's breakfast, they were paddling downstream on the Black. Since it was a known canoe route, triangular yellow signs identified designated portages around rapids. Harry and James, in the front canoe, found they could run most of the rapids, which was more fun and easier than hauling the vessel out across a woodland trail. Whenever a portage sign was spotted, they approached the rapids slowly, assessed the turbulence of the water and decided whether to paddle through or get out and carry around. Jim and Corry, in the second canoe, followed their sons' lead. At one point the second canoe overtook the first.

The channel ahead narrowed between sloping rock outcrops, with a roar of larger rapids ahead. Jim did not notice the portage sign on the left side. As the canoe was entering the channel, Corry nervously wobbled side to side in the front seat. Water spilled in over the gunnels, then gushed in, and the canoe tipped over. Corry fell out to the left, then instinctively grabbed onto the protruding outcrop on the side of the channel. Jim slipped out and swam for shore. The canoe, now full of water, kept on going straight through. Moments later they heard a terrible crack and the sound of tumbling fibreglass. James and Harry nosed their canoe into where the portage sign directed them, then helped Corry out of the water. They were astounded at what they saw at the end of the portage. Not merely rapids, but a vertical three-metre drop of churning water with a busted blue canoe lying at the base. If Corry had not tipped the canoe where she did, the two of them would have gone straight over the waterfalls with more serious consequences. They would not be paddling any further in that boat. How had Jim and James missed seeing the waterfalls when they did their aerial reconnaissance?

CHAPTER 15

The Kids in Their Teenage Years

All parents face challenges when raising children. New mothers and fathers have their own parents as role models, but new situations arise that the previous generation never had. Jim's heavy-handed father was his example which no doubt influenced his approach to fatherhood. Corry too, had been raised to have the utmost respect and not question her parents. Spankings and harsh discipline were just how children were kept in line. As a result, Jim, and to a lesser extent Corry, took a fairly strict approach to raising their three boys. Jim as the unquestionable head of the household, was used to making unilateral decisions, demanded full respect and did not put up with backtalk. Such an approach may work fine with young children but is less effective once they grow into the rebellious teenage years.

Jim also demanded that his boys grow up with a strong work ethic. There would be no lazy kids in this family! Running the landscape business and later, the garden centre, ensured that there were always tasks to be done. When only eight-years-old, James and Harry were given hoes and ordered to work up the soil and knock down weeds among the many rows of nursery trees. They griped about toiling in the hot sun while their friends played but later learned there were many less pleasant jobs. Weekly mopping the floor of the office and store was one. Bare-rooted shrubs were trucked in and these needed to be potted. Often after coming home from school, James and Harry worked together, filling endless bags with shredded topsoil that would be sold to customers.

Sometimes there were nastier jobs like applying creosote to railway ties, picking stones from the field, or digging holes. Once they reached the age of twelve, the boys were made to work every Saturday. Sometimes they would assist Jim in residential landscaping jobs.

Jim and James with a baled Christmas tree.

Jim taught them to pay attention to the job at hand to spot and do the obvious tasks.

"Don't just stand there and wait to be told. Just get in there and do it," he would say.

Jim taught them how to level soil with a rake, lay sod evenly, prune shrubs, lay patio slabs, workup flower beds, and how to form a burlap ball around the base of a large tree. He was not the most patient teacher, though, the kids had to learn fast. Jim's main philosophies are embodied in his frequently stated words of wisdom:

"Always stick up for your family."
"Finish whatever job you start."
"Clean up after yourself."
"Don't just try, do it!"
"Don't cheat the customer or anyone else."
"Once you've made your decision, stick by it."
"Never be late."
"You'll never get rich if you work for someone else."

On occasion, one of the boys would accompany Jim along with a couple of labourers to dig up cedars. Jim would make a deal with a farmer to dig up cedar saplings from a piece of rough pasture. Mostly 1 to 2 metres in height, cedars were easy to dig with a sharp spade as they had a surprisingly small and shallow root system and usually grew on moist ground. Beads of sweat dripped from the brows of all workers, between digging, carrying trees, and loading the spindly cedars onto the truck. The trees were taken to job sites to be planted in rows forming instant cedar hedges or taken back to the garden centre.

Jim could take a task and complete it with remarkable efficiency. He was not afraid to work hard, and none of his workers could match him. A customer's yard could consist of a monotonous plot of only grass in the morning. By day's end, the property had been transformed. It now held colourful flower beds, tastefully arranged shrub plantings, scattered ornamental trees and a laid-out patio.

James recalled a time when a customer approached him to say, "Wow, that dad of yours sure can work. I have never seen anyone work as fast."

At the start of a job, Jim would decide how best to tackle it, usually without a lot of pondering or need to consider options. Once he set his mind, he just did it. He was a hard act to follow for his sons. How could they ever live up to their father? Jim's focus on getting a job done efficiently often made him reluctant to listen to another's point of view or advice, especially when that viewpoint came from one of his sons.

Against such a backdrop, it is not surprising that some familial conflicts arose. Jim had rebelled against his strict father, so what could he expect? His "do as I say" approach led to tension when the boys became old enough to question his authority. Teenagers are not known for their infinite wisdom either. Sometimes they just must strike out to achieve their own independence and face their own consequences.

One of the issues was hair. These were the early 1970s when nearly all teenage boys liked to grow their hair over their ears and preferably down to their shoulders. Jim found the look of long hair on males very irritating. Perhaps it represented lazy, drug-using, and rebellious hippies. No way were his kids going to become "long hairs."

Whenever he noticed that the blonde strands started creeping over their ears, James, Harry, and Ted were ordered off to the barber to get it snipped. The boys would put up a fuss, but it did no good. Barber Andy must have felt awkward, seeing the disgruntled lads coming in for a clip they did not want. Over time, however, the boy's hair gradually lengthened, and Jim made less of a fuss about it. He must have realized that he was not going to win this one, or maybe Corry played a role in softening his view. Another issue was that the boys had to work every weekend, while their friends were off having fun. However, if the boys came up strong with good reasons and compromises to get a free Saturday, Jim would cut them some slack.

A parent must do their best to raise and protect their offspring, even when it means dragging them off to get unwanted haircuts which he believed might prevent them from associating with the "wrong kind". Jim took this role very seriously. Although he came across as uncompromising to his sons, Jim would do almost anything to defend them, including "bend the rules" if required. His three sons were no angels and found their way into trouble on occasion. At age 17, James and his 16-year-old friend Mark Saunders went out for the night to a teen dance in Oshawa. The boys were in good spirits, having consumed several beers each before showing up at the hall. A policeman noticed them clowning around on the street so asked them to come over and breathe in his face.

"You boys have been drinking, haven't you? How old are you? Let's have some I.D.," the officer demanded.

There was no point denying it. James and Mark were charged with underage drinking, as the legal age at the time was 18. They were each issued a summons.

Several weeks later, the boys put on their finest suits and appeared in an Oshawa courtroom accompanied by Jim and Mark's dad, Allan. Jim fabricated a story that the boys had indulged in a couple of beers with the other workers after a hard day on the job at Kamstra Landscaping. The judge fell for the story, and the charges were dropped.

A couple of years later, Ted had a similar charge of under-age drinking. He was on the front yard of where a house party was taking place when the police stopped by, perhaps responding to a "disturbing of the peace" complaint from a disgruntled neighbour. Ted admitted to drinking so he was summoned. Jim and Ted dressed up for this court case as well. Judge Dodds, who presided over the case, was one of Jim's landscaping customers which may have helped for that case was also dismissed.

In February 1976, Jim and Corry decided to travel to Europe for a month. The boys were all in high school with James in his final year, so it was not good for him to take that much time off. They both felt it unwise to leave three unsupervised teenage boys alone in the house. James at 18 and 16-year-old Harry were trusted to stay home to look after the place. Rebellious Ted was in no mood for a free trip to Europe with his parents, but he was dragged along, nonetheless.

The three flew to the Netherlands, which entailed obligatory visits to many relatives. The parents could see that sipping coffee in the living rooms and yammering away in Dutch with old folks was not very stimulating for a disgruntled teenager.

To make the trip more bearable, Jim purchased a used Vespa scooter which Ted could cruise around town as he pleased, during the "boring" visits. Ted tested the limits of the bike as he raced through narrow cobbled streets and on paths through the countryside. Dutch signs were confusing, roads often indirect, and he had no map to navigate, so he made sure to pay close attention to his routes to avoid getting lost. Ted was a little sad to have to sell the scooter when they left Holland.

The parents with son in tow, boarded a southbound train from Amsterdam to Paris, then another to Madrid and a third to Lisbon, Portugal. Jim had hired many Portuguese workers over the years. Most were migrants who flew to Canada, worked hard to earn cash in the warm months, then returned to the leisurely pace of Portugal for the winter. One worker who stood out among the rest, Salvador Ganhao, a loyal and diligent employee who toiled for many seasons at Kamstra Landscaping. He was Jim's favourite and was more than just an employee, he was a friend. When they appeared at the door, Salvador and his wife welcomed the Kamstras with open arms. Salvador invited them to stay several days and proudly showed them around his country.

They rented a small car to tour around Portugal. On occasion, Jim let Ted drive through medieval streets and curvy roads of the countryside, despite the fact he was fifteen and unlicensed. At one point, when Jim drove through a particularly narrow street, their car scraped against a parked car. Bystanders yelled out and shook their fists in the air. Not speaking the language, he feared a bureaucratic nightmare with local police and what the townspeople might accuse him of. He kept on driving. A few days later, Jim, Corry, and Ted were buckled in their seats on the flight back to Toronto.

Meanwhile, back in Oshawa, it was the last weekend of that frigid month, and two days before the parents were due back from Europe. James held a house party for some of his friends. With no parents around to chaperone, what could go wrong? The trouble was his friends told their friends, who told other friends, and before long word got out that there was an open party at the Kamstra house. Cars started showing up, one after another. The plowed garden centre parking lot beside the house could accommodate dozens of cars. The lot filled up and other vehicles parked on the roadside. Scruffy teenagers of various descriptions came into the house carrying cases of beer. Many of them James didn't know. They were not from his school, and he did not have the sense to turn people away.

Over a hundred people crowded into the house. Guests, if you can call them that, could barely move between rooms. The situation was out of control. Some entered the parent's bedroom, jumped on the bed and it collapsed. A closet door came off its hinges and a lamp fell crashing to the floor. Other careless, intoxicated patrons dropped lit cigarette butts onto the carpet. Several personal items, including works of art, just disappeared that night. James finally screamed that the party was over and ordered everyone to leave. A few friends returned the next day to help vacuum floors, shampoo carpets, and dispose of bottles, but there was no way of hiding the evidence.

Jim blew up and Corry was outright shocked when they saw the condition of their home. How could this happen as they thought that James was the most responsible one of their boys. James felt remorseful and was apologetic and tried to make amends. Harry, on the other hand, was defiant. It wasn't his party, after all. He had nothing to do with it. The boys tried to explain this, but Jim would not listen. In the coming weeks, Harry and Jim had several arguments with strong words flinging back and forth. Neither would see the other person's point of view. Harry finally proclaimed, "the hell with this, I'm outta here!"

He packed up a few clothes and walked out the door, then moved in with a buddy named Chuck and his family. Then long-time friend, Jim Ruigrok, invited Harry to stay with his family for a time. After a couple of months, he felt that welcome wore off, so he found another friend who would take him in. Harry transferred from Courtice Secondary School to a city school, Donevan Collegiate, to complete his high schooling. The whole ordeal was probably hardest on Corry who did not see her son for months, the only contact through sporadic phone calls. Corry invited Harry to join the family for Thanksgiving dinner. With cooler heads, Harry was able to resolve issues with his father and before long moved back in with the family.

Harry at age 17.

Meanwhile, Ted had his own adventures. One Friday night in the autumn of 1976, when Jim and Corry were out for the evening, Ted decided to take the company-owned Jeep out for a joy ride with a couple of his friends. The unlicensed 15year-old sped recklessly along backroads and had gone about ten kilometres before losing control and slamming the vehicle head-on into a tree. Fortunately, no one was hurt. Not knowing what else to do, Ted and his friends ran away from the scene without reporting it. Ted stayed over at the home of one of his partners in crime.

The next morning Jim received a phone call from Durham Regional Police stating that a wrecked Jeep belonging to Kamstra Landscaping was found abandoned. Jim proclaimed to know nothing about it and reported that the vehicle had been stolen from the premises. After a serious interrogation by his father, Ted admitted that indeed he had taken and cracked up the pickup. Although Jim did not divulge this information to the police, they had obtained evidence that the Kamstra boy was the culprit. Jim feared that Ted, who was already faring poorly at school and lacking direction, would continue on a downward spiral if charged and sent to jail or reformed school. Since it was Jim's vehicle and he did not press charges, Ted did not suffer any repercussions. Among his punishments, Jim would not let Ted apply for a driver's licence until he was 17.

The family soon went through another traumatic event involving vehicles. Like his uncle of the same name, Harry had an affinity for fast foreign convertibles, so he bought himself a used 1971 Triumph Spitfire. He loved that little blue speedster and could be seen zipping it around town. The sporty machine was not designed for winter conditions, however, with its low clearance and draftiness due to the rubbery retractable roof. Nevertheless, Harry drove it through all kinds of weather. Shifting gears and accelerating on snowy roads were no problem, he had plenty of horsepower under the hood.

In December 1977, Harry showed up at a tobogganing party at the big hill near Enniskillen, meeting up with a bunch of high school friends. At the end of the fun afternoon, he hopped in the Spitfire and raced home along icy roads. Somewhere along Townline Road, the vehicle hit some ice, swerved one way then the other and completely lost control. With a terrible thud, it slammed head-on into something hard. Time seemed to stop as Harry blacked out.

The rest of the family were sitting in the Taunton home, settling in after another one of Corry's exquisite home cooked suppers. The phone rang. Jim picked it up.

"There's been an accident. Your son is in the hospital."

The parents and brothers jumped in the family car and headed to Oshawa General Hospital. They were allowed into the emergency room where they saw Harry sprawled out unconscious with bandages covering much of his face, hiding his broken teeth. Bottles of clear liquid on a metal stand connected intravenous tubes to his arms; wires extended from his chest to electronic monitors. It was bad. The doctor was not confident that he would pull out of it. Harry laid unconscious like this for several days.

Then Harry came to, confused, confined, and experiencing indescribable pain. At least he was alive! He could not remember a thing about the accident. Several days after gaining consciousness, an agent from the car insurance company showed up at Harry's bedside. Speaking sincerely, the agent promised prompt payments if Harry would just sign a couple of forms. Harry was in no condition to interpret the fine print. He just accepted that the kind gentleman was looking after his best interests, so he signed. Jim later found out that the papers would limit the company's liability of payments for the required dental reconstruction and other costs. Jim filed a claim and took the company to court. The papers were withdrawn.

Harry's Triumph Spitfire after the accident.

Harry spent ten days on recovery in the hospital. Young nurses who attended him admired the tall handsome patient, injured, but in his prime of life. Little by little, the healing process worked. Once out of hospital, Harry underwent weeks of rehab, but his healthy body eventually pulled him through for a full recovery. He finally felt well enough to return to Donevan Collegiate. Continual intense headaches made it hard to concentrate or study, however. Nevertheless, he persevered and was able to graduate from his final year of high school.

CHAPTER 16

Inviting Brother Sid into the Business

Having lived his life in the Netherlands, Sietse was curious about Canada. What was it about the place that had lured away his two older brothers? He would see for himself. With his wife, Wiesje, and their two children in tow, Sietse came for a month visit to Canada in the summer of 1974, their first time to North America. That experience was all the family could have hoped. Jim, Corry, and family were so welcoming. Sietse marvelled at how his brother fit into his adopted land and had created a small empire.

As is customary, they visited family but also took in the natural wonders of Niagara Falls and Algonquin Park, and Jim gave them the keys to the Trent River cottage for a week. Yes, Canada is the life! The wide-open spaces, warm summer weather, and lifestyle appealed to Sietse. The visit also had a profound effect on Sietse's 11-year-old son, Jimmy. He admired his dynamic namesake uncle and hoped to follow in his footsteps in Canada one day. Vacation over, they returned to their normal lives in Holland.

A year or so later, Jim was trying to find the right manager for the garden centre. He wanted to focus his efforts on landscape contracts and the expanding topsoil ends of the business. He just could not find a suitable garden centre manager, at least not since Dorothy Shade had resigned. Then it occurred to Jim that who could be better than family! What about Sietse and Wiesje? They owned and operated a successful fruit and vegetable store called "Happy Fruit Corner" in the town of Meppel. Sietse had all the required business skills. He knew all about ordering stock, displaying goods, keeping track of inventory, financial responsibility and customer service. His friendly nature and ability to make people feel good were a real asset for handling customers. But could he be persuaded?

Jim made Sietse an offer to become a partner in the Kamstra Landscaping business. Maybe not quite an equal partner since Jim started the company and had so much invested. Nevertheless, what a rare and exciting opportunity, in Canada! Sietse became excited with the prospect but first had to convince Wiesje. Then they had to consider how it would affect the children, Jimmy and Simone. New country, new language, new school, and of course new friends. Fortunately, Dutch schools taught compulsory English, so the young siblings had a basic familiarity with the language.

There would be logistic hurdles. Dutch immigrants were not accepted so readily as they had been twenty years earlier. Jim had to sponsor the family and prove that Sietse would have guaranteed employment and that he possessed essential skills that were not readily available in the Canadian population. Sietse meanwhile travelled to the Canadian Consulate in the Hague for an interview, proving that he had sufficient financial resources and a level of fluency in English.

But what would he do with the Happy Fruit Corner? The store was popular among the Meppel townsfolk and would fetch a reasonable price if listed on the market. Instead, Sietse transferred the business over to Douwe, the last Kamstra sibling who still resided in the Netherlands. Douwe was the produce manager for DeBoer's, a Dutch grocery franchise, so he intimately knew this line of business. He also had the same friendly flair for customer service as his brother. It was Douwe's chance to get ahead, to run his own show. Along with his wife, Dina, Douwe successfully operated and even grew the Happy Fruit Corner for the next several years. However, their marriage hit a rocky road, and they divorced. The store would suffer the same fate. It went through a period of decline, then went bankrupt, to shut down for good.

On June 6, 1976, Sietse's family arrived in Canada with whatever belongings they could import. In the Kamstra tradition of anglicizing given names, Sietse became "Sid," just as Tjebbe had become "Jim." Wiesje became "Wendy." The children, Jimmy and Simone, already had suitably anglicized names that needed no adjustment. The family crowded in with Jim and Corry's family for their first six weeks in the country then purchased a comfortable house with a spacious yard in the hamlet of Mitchell's Corners, only a couple kilometres east of the Kamstra Landscaping garden centre.

Sid and Wendy adapted well in the new land and together ran all aspects of the garden centre. Sid's charm and natural chattiness made him a favourite with the customers. He had a knack for being able to sell. Wendy, a little more reserved, was hesitant at first with the fast-speaking Canadians and struggled to develop English fluency. Nevertheless, Wendy learned to enjoy interacting with customers, tending to plants, and especially being able to work alongside her husband.

The kids started classes at Mitchell's Corners Public School that September. Jimmy, an outgoing lad, joined a local soccer team and made new friends almost immediately. By contrast, little Simone did not take to the new country so quickly. She missed her old friends and as she struggled with English, she had a hard time making new ones. With time she adapted and became so Canadianized that after several years lost much of her command of Dutch.

Sid became a legal part-owner of Kamstra Landscaping in 1978. To learn more about this new trade, Sid enrolled in a landscape training course offered at Durham College over the winter of 1976 -77. A government sponsored course was taught by Jim's main competitor and one-time rival, Rene Thiebaud, owner of Oshawa Garden Service.

Jim and Rene avoided each other, but both shared a common history of coming from Europe with very little and building up successful businesses through sheer hard work. They shared a mutual level of respect. The program did not offer a college diploma but was a practical oriented course covering many aspects of the landscape business based on Rene's personal experience. James enrolled along with Sid, since he also worked in the family business, and was contemplating landscaping as a possible career.

Morley Travis with Sid and Jim holding up large spruce Christmas tree.

CHAPTER 17

Sons in the Business

Almost from Kamstra Landscaping's inception, Jim foresaw that one day all three of his sons would work at, and eventually run, the business that he created. Like it or not, the boys were exposed at a young age, first helping out on Saturdays or occasional days during the summer holidays. James started working full time in the summer of 1972 at the age of 14. He worked mostly with the grounds-maintenance foreman, Rennie Bassie: cutting grass, cultivating flowerbeds, and generally looking after the yards of wealthy customers. Harry and Ted did the same when they reached that age.

The value of hard work was instilled upon them. Once finished high school in the late 1970s, all three sons were on the company payroll, yet none were showing real leadership.

What's wrong with those boys, thought Jim. *Their future is laid out for them. The hard work of starting a business has been done.*

Rennie Bassie had left Kamstra Landscaping to start his own company early in 1977. James and Harry were put in charge of the grounds maintenance division that had been Rennie's domain. They worked well and did what was needed. Still, the brothers would not rise to the challenge of learning the inner workings of the business and taking on real responsibility. They left that up to their dynamic dad.

James was more interested in pursuing a life in the natural sciences than the business of landscaping. However, he had a general disinterest in post-secondary education following his lacklustre performance during his final year of high school. After a couple of years out of school and travelling abroad to Australia, James realized that without higher education, his options would be limited. He applied to Trent University to study biology and environmental science. Jim urged him also to take some business management courses that would be applicable. James sat in on an introductory lecture on business administration, but it did not stimulate his interest; he did not enroll.

Harry fell into a period of soul searching after high school. He wasn't so sure that a life in landscaping was for him either, but he had no other fall-back plan. A new government sponsored program called Katimavik sounded interesting. Created by Prime Minister Pierre Trudeau, Katimavik gave participating youth the opportunity to live and work in various locations across Canada to experience life in a cross-section of the country. Harry would have to commit to nine months away from home, which was fine by him.

Between 1979 and 1980, he spent three month-long stints at three locations: the interior mountains near Nelson B.C., along the north shore of the St. Lawrence River in Sault-au-Mouton, Quebec, and in Prince Edward Island. Harry lived with local families, worked at non-profit organizations, learned about living sustainably and independently. He also learned basic French and how to cook.

Harry (centre) with others in the Katimavik program in Quebec.

He came back a changed man, with improved morale and a renewed sense of purpose. He decided that landscaping was a noble career worth pursuing and enrolled in a three-year landscape technology program at Humber College in Toronto. Harry already knew much about this field; he grew up with it. Whether by instruction or just exposure, he had learned much from his father. Jim never took formal training in landscaping, he just figured out a way that worked with each new task. Harry, on the other hand, would get the proper certification, essential for dealing working in an ever more regulated world. He learned about suitable plant materials and where they were best suited, soil, fertilizers, building materials, operation of equipment, landscape design, drafting, and business management. He graduated from the college in 1983 with a Diploma in Landscape Technology.

Harry then took on a more determined role in business operations. He developed a different approach than that of his father. Jim could meet a customer, listen to their desires, look at the layout of the yard then come up with a quick sketch and cost estimate in half an hour. Harry was more meticulous. First, he would start a discussion to find out what the customer wanted, then look at a yard to visualize different arrangements of plantings, rock gardens, retaining walls or patios. Back at the office, he would draft up a scaled plan and prepare an itemized cost estimate.

Harry's life was about to change in other ways. He met Joni Cassar, a petite dark-haired woman of Maltese descent in the winter of 1986. Like Harry, she was also a skier. They soon developed strong feelings for each other and became a couple. Two years later, they made their vows at a Catholic church in Courtice, followed by a grand family reception. Harry and Joni moved into the house on one of Jim's properties that previously held tenants. In August 1991, Joni gave birth to Jessica Marie Kamstra, the first grandchild for Jim and Corry, a girl in this mostly male family. A second child, Erik Joseph, came into their lives two years later. By this time, however, a wedge had formed between the once amiable couple. Some differences could not be resolved. Harry and Joni separated, then Harry moved out.

Ted too, was not sure that landscaping was his calling, but he worked summers at Kamstra Landscaping during high school, then year-round when done with school. He never had to look for a job, and he made as much cash as he needed. He continued to live with his folks at 1470 Taunton Road where his meals and accommodation were looked after.

But in the spring of 1982, Ted had a desire to try something else, and somewhere else. The only place he had ever worked was the family business. He had never created a resume nor applied anywhere else. Furthermore, his hometown of Oshawa struck him as a place without character. To put it mildly, it was boring. Why not try…California, now that sounded like an exciting place to be! How many had gone before and found their fortunes there? Ted packed some clothes, a sleeping bag and a few other items which he tossed into the trunk of his FIAT automobile. He drove the interstate highways west across the United States for several days before reaching Los Angeles.

Finding work at farms and factories was easy enough. Employers were mostly looking for unskilled labour with no questions asked. Ted appeared strong and healthy, so he was readily hired. Ted never applied for a US work permit as he did not qualify and, therefore, was technically illegal. He introduced himself as "Ned Kenstre" whenever applying for work. By using a false social security number, cheques from short-term employers could be cashed. After a few odd jobs and dealings with questionable characters, California did not seem so rosy anymore.

He learned that there was a high demand for tree planters on the barren slopes of Mount St. Helens in Washington state. He loaded his belongings in the FIAT then headed north from the Golden State. The scenery surrounding the dormant volcano was breathtaking, but the planting job backbreaking. Hauling sacks of seedlings up steep, unvegetated slopes and digging into the rocky ground paid well as long as you could put a lot of trees in the earth. A couple of paychecks later, Ted left the states and crossed back into Canada. In Vancouver, thieves broke into Ted's car and stole some items and that was enough; he was ready to come home after five months away. Back to work at Kamstra Landscaping, Ted was still not entirely committed to it.

The following summer Ted tried a second stint in the west, but this time stayed on the Canadian side; he went to Edmonton, Alberta, where he could at least work legally. This time he rode west on his motorcycle. Since his credentials were limited, he accepted whatever company would hire him. With the building boom, he toiled in a construction crew and then tried driving as a mail courier. At last, he was hired to do the kind of work that he knew well, for a company called Park Landscaping Ltd. Although he started as a regular labourer, the boss soon promoted Ted to foreman, impressed with his experience and hardworking ability. Ted led his work crew on various jobs through the prairie summer.

Ted with his loaded motorcycle ready to ride out west.

In the autumn, the boss offered him a hefty raise if he would stay on. Ted pondered the opportunity but not for long; he had enough of Alberta. He found it colder, less secure, and generally a rougher place to be than Ontario. Maybe Oshawa wasn't such a boring place after all! He resigned from Park, packed up his stuff, and motored back eastward on the Trans-Canada Highway. Back in Oshawa, he completed the landscape course at Durham College that was still being taught by Rene Thiebaud, then took a renewed interest in Kamstra Landscaping.

Ted took command of his own group of labourers to undertake some of the larger jobs. He could work hard and motivate his crew to complete a project on time. Still, he did not have the finesse for completing multifaceted residential jobs that involved various specialized tasks. Harry could look after those. Ted did not have a keen interest in plants and did not have a good sense of what species were most suited to a particular purpose or location. Instead, he had an affinity for engines, for operating and fixing them. Types of jobs where Ted could shine included large sodding jobs in new subdivisions, boulevard tree plantings, operating excavators, grading with tractors, trucking and working soil.

Harry and Ted had finally 'seen the light,' ready to take their rightful place at the helm of the business. Jim was happy to see this turnaround. He called a meeting of the four Kamstras in late 1985 to negotiate a working business arrangement. He envisioned that they would work out an amenable four-way partnership. However, Sid and Jim's sons did not have a congenial nor cooperative working relationship. Even with Jim acting as mediator, he was not able to get them to formulate a workable agreement. By the end of the meeting, Jim, Harry and Ted became the partners of Kamstra Landscaping. Sid became owner and operator of the Kamstra Garden Centre and greenhouse, which entailed the merchandise, inventory and actual business. The buildings and land remained part of Kamstra Landscaping. Two separate companies would now operate out of the same building. Jim and Corry and sons were quite happy to be free of the garden centre.

Sid and Wendy ran an organized operation for about ten years over which time they bought and sold a great quantity of box plants, shrubs, fertilizers, garden tools, lawn ornaments and Christmas trees, among other things. Always a smile, ever helpful and showing genuine interest in the people he served, Sid developed a loyal following of customers, and the store thrived. Their daughter Simone worked in the store when old enough, while Jimmy, employed at GM, helped out on weekends. No doubt, increasing competition from the big stores was becoming a bigger challenge. Department stores, Canadian Tire, and virtually every grocery store put up seasonal garden centres on the side, selling potted plants, and gardening goods. With convenience and better prices due to volume, many former customers were now purchasing their gardening supplies at the big conglomerates.

Jimmy Kamstra, Chris and Sid unloading nursery stock from cube van, spring 1989.

Wendy Kamstra trimming plants in the garden centre, 1989.

Sid and Wendy tried new products and maintained sufficient sales to keep the business profitable. Whether it was worry about increasing competition, too much lifting or other sources of stress, Sid eventually developed a chronic sore shoulder. He no longer enjoyed the garden centre. Having two independent businesses operating on the same turf was, at times, awkward. Dump trucks moving about, customer parking, storing of materials and alterations to buildings created occasional friction between Kamstra Landscaping and the garden centre. Enough was enough! A combination of factors convinced Sid and Wendy to take an early retirement prior to the year 2000.

Seeing that his job was on the line, their store assistant Tom asked if he could take over and administer Kamstra Garden Centre. Tom worked out an arrangement with both Sid and Jim then assumed ownership. He ran the operation along with his wife and son. It seemed to be working for several months, but the young couple lacked the organizational skills and suave approach with the customers that Sid had. Within a year, the garden centre was in trouble. Sales were plummeting, and the bookkeeping was in disarray. Tom left, leaving a pile of unpaid debts to suppliers. Kamstra Garden Centre was back in the hands of Kamstra Landscaping. Corry was particularly upset in having the store tossed back into their lap. She had spent her years running the store decades ago and was not about to go back to the stress and long hours that it required.

Maybe it was time for the sons to manage the garden centre. Ted only had to think about it for one minute before concluding that he did not have the inclination, finesse, nor patience for dealing with customers and the bewildering amount of merchandise in the store. It was up to Harry then. Fortunately, he had found a cheerful partner who might rise to the task.

Ever since he was a teenager, Harry was an avid downhill skier. Once the low hills of Ontario resorts offered little challenge, he found the longer and higher vertical runs of central British Columbia more to his liking. Every winter he took an extended skiing vacation to Rossland, B.C., a place he knew well. On one trip in February 1997, he met Debbie Kummer, a pretty blonde from Stoney Creek, Ontario, who stayed at the same hotel. They could chat easily and soon found that they had much in common and continued to see each other back in Ontario. One thing led to another; feelings grew.

Debbie recalled the first time she met Harry's parents when invited for dinner. She liked Jim from the start. He was charming, curious and friendly, but also a little intimidating and opinionated. Corry was less forthright but welcoming, and wow, could she whip up a savoury Dutch meal. Debbie was impressed.

Debbie understood the complexities of a family business. Her father, Tom Kummer, and an uncle operated Idlewood Trucking, a company that was started by her grandfather. For almost a decade, Debbie managed the company office, took orders, prepared invoices, and attended to various business logistics. Then one day in 2000, Tom decided that he had worked long enough and was ready to retire. The brothers dissolved Idlewood Trucking and Debbie was out of a job.

With nothing keeping her in Stoney Creek, she pulled up stakes and moved in with Harry at 1470 Taunton Road, Oshawa. She intended to find meaningful employment in this unfamiliar but bustling city. She applied at various companies and looked for leads but no-one would hire her. Maybe she just needed to get current and upgrade her skills. She enrolled in several computer and accounting courses at the local college. Debbie was now ready for a new career managing the garden centre at Kamstras.

Debbie eased her way into the business. Not only would she be living with Harry, but also working with him, a real trial for the new relationship. And if it did not work out, then what? She would give it her very best.

Botany was not something Debbie knew much about. With more than his usual patience, Jim taught her about different plant materials and where they would fit into a garden. Flowering shrubs, annuals, biennials, perennials, deciduous and coniferous in so many colours and shapes. There were peonies, geraniums, begonias, roses, spireas, junipers and forsythias. Some for sun, some for shade, and some for semi-shade. Debbie paid attention and caught on quickly.

Other times Jim was not so patient. One her tasks was daily watering the rows and rows of potted plants with hose and nozzle. A seemingly simple task, but Jim could not hold back his comments if he felt the job could be done better. Debbie sometimes got heck for over-watering, and sometimes for under watering plants. Debbie certainly received no special treatment because she was the son's girlfriend. But when a job was done well, Jim would be full of praise. At least Debbie knew where she stood and did not have to second guess with Jim.

Harry with Debbie Kummer.

Other staff helped in the store through the busy season, and Corry worked in the office or store two days a week. The garden centre was becoming more and more the domain of Harry and Debbie, but only to a point. Jim always started the workday meeting with all staff in the office. He needed to know what staff were doing and to make sure that no important tasks were missed. He would fire out questions and commands to set the pace, then head out to do other tasks. This approach raised the blood pressure of any staff that were present, especially Harry and Debbie. They could not make any significant changes in running the garden centre without Jim's grace. Jim would question quantities of stock orders or if they wanted to try selling a new item in the store.

"Don't order that stuff," he would say. "It will never sell."

Debbie felt frustrated.

Nevertheless, Debbie ordered a large number of watering cans and various planters without consulting Jim. When the delivery truck arrived with a stack of cardboard boxes, she thought, "oh-oh, Jim is not going to like this!"

Harry and Debbie quickly moved the boxes into the basement of their house, where Jim would not see them. The watering cans and planters were discreetly moved to the store in small batches as they sold. Jim never made a fuss because he never caught on.

Despite occasional heated arguments between Debbie and Jim about business matters, they mostly got along and worked well together. Debbie knew how family relations could deteriorate if they let disagreements get personal. She would get annoyed at Jim but could always see the positive side while maintaining a forgiving disposition. Jim would apologize when he realized he pushed too far, or he would soon forget the issue. Grudges were never held for long.

Although legally Kamstra Landscaping had become a three-way partnership between Harry, Ted and Jim, in practice, it did not operate that way. Jim was still very much in control, making most of the business decisions. Maybe he feared that the boys could not run things as efficiently as he, and they were not managing things the way that he would. Perhaps he saw that they lacked the kind drive and determination that he had at their age. Very few people do. Maybe it was just in Jim's nature that he always had to be the one in charge.

Harry would sometimes challenge one of Jim's decisions or vice versa, and the two would butt heads. Jim would sometimes back down but usually not. His word was usually final. Ted, on the other hand, rarely challenged Jim, was generally content to let his father talk on and have his way. After all, Jim had decades of experience running a successful business and Ted was not about to challenge what seemed to be working.

Front of Kamstra Garden Centre in 2006.

CHAPTER 18

If It's Not from Kamstra's, It's Just Dirt

Soil is the essential medium that rooted plants require, and therefore is a critical consideration for anyone in the business of growing plants. Jim understood that suitable or sufficient soil was often not present where people wanted their gardens, which is why good soil became such an integral part of Kamstra Landscaping. Compared to landscaping or operating the garden centre, dealing with soil was a simple business. Truck material in, mix and screen it, sell it, and truck it out to customers. Not much involved with preparing the product. All that was needed were a ready supply of it, a place to stockpile it, and some big machines to work it: front-end loaders, soil shredders, and dump trucks. Jim saw this niche market and was not shy about investing in whatever was needed.

Nearly every landscape job, big or small, needed topsoil. It was Jim's job to find it. Topsoil mostly came from construction sites. Developers would strip and stockpile the topsoil from land before houses could be constructed. Only a small amount of the soil would be returned to the lots for lawns once the new homes were completed. Generally, soil piles were just in the way and a nuisance to developers. Sometimes Jim drove around the outskirts of town looking for sites where residential homes were approved, and excavation had begun. He would find out who the developer was and contact them to make a deal. Often, they were happy to get rid of it and would sell it for a song. Sometimes they let Jim have the "pile of dirt" for the trouble of trucking it away. Jim would have a front-end loader trailered into the site, then send in his drivers with tandem or split-axle dump trucks to haul the stuff back to the yard.

Jim approached horse or cattle farmers to obtain manure, rich in nitrogen and other nutrients needed for healthy plants. Jim was a shrewd wheeler-dealer, trying to get the smelly stuff for the best price he could. Sometimes he got it for free and at least once, the farmer actually paid him to haul the precious resource away. Some farmers scooped the manure out of the styles and piled it outside of their barn where it might sit for years.

"It is not a wise farmer who gives away his manure," Jim once said to James. "A smart farmer knows to spread it on his fields. It's free fertilizer."

Jim preferred dealing with dumb farmers.

The third critical element in Kamstra's famous "triple mix" was peat loam, the rich black organics that form from dead and decomposing trees in the saturated ground of wetlands. This Jim obtained from rural swampy properties that he bought just for that purpose. He would have his workers cut down the trees then hire a dragline with an operator to scoop the sloppy black material out of the water, creating ponds in the process. The piles were left to dry out for a few weeks before the tandems came to pick it up. His salvaged swamps could be fifty kilometres away. All of the material was transported back to the Kamstra Landscaping yard in an untold number of truckloads.

An ever-changing mountain range of stockpiled material was created behind the barn on the Kamstra Landscaping property. A front-end loader dumped lumpy soil into the greedy mouth of the shredder, where it was first hammered then rolled through a cylindrical screen. It was pulverized into a powdery workable medium that customers could easily apply to their gardens. A great conveyor belt

Jim operating front-end loader at a soil pile.

sent a never-ending line of earth diagonally upward, then dropping it into pyramidal piles.

For years Kamstra had a virtual monopoly of topsoil in the Oshawa area. The office phone rang off the hook with orders, especially through spring, with requests for deliveries to residences all around Oshawa and beyond. Jim fashioned a laneway so that trucks could bypass the garden centre to the stockpiles in the back. Kamstra's half dozen dump trucks rarely sat idle. The driver would run in the office to pick up a paper order form, drive to the back, wait for the loader to fill the box, then drive off to the customer. Other customers lined up with pickups or cars pulling trailers. Most other landscaper contractors and many garden centres came to Kamstra Landscaping to get their soil. Debbie came up with a catchy advertising slogan that would be used in newspaper and local radio commercials, "If it's not soil from Kamstra's, it's just plain dirt."

Aerial view of Kamstra Landscaping and Garden Centre in 2012 showing soil piles in the back.

The adjacent 20-hectare property to the west, long owned by Don Welch, came up for sale in 2006. Such an opportunity was not likely to happen again, so Jim pounced on it. He made an offer that was accepted, thereby increasing his land holdings threefold. The new parcel had limited potential for development. A headwater branch of Harmony Creek bisected the property, and much of it lay within the floodplain, where municipal regulations forbade the erection of buildings. Still, it was immediately next door. Jim could expand the topsoil storage area, as well as plant more nursery stock.

In the early 2000s, as Jim got older, and began slowing down just a bit, he mostly confined himself to organizing the soil component, which had become the most lucrative part of the business. Harry and Ted could take care of the landscaping and the garden centre. Even at age 85, Jim was operating the excavator, mixing soil and stockpiling. He still loved the hum of working machinery among the stockpiles and the bustle of empty trucks driving in then leaving with full loads of black gold.

At one point, Jim gave some fatherly advice to Harry and Ted, "Why don't you get out of landscaping? It's a young man's business, too rough on the body. Why not stick with the garden centre and soil?"

No doubt, landscaping was a punishing career on the body. All three men had gone through bouts of back pain so severe that they needed to take time off work and undergo chiropractic therapy. The job involved digging, heavy lifting, bending and frequent twisting of the torso. The work may have been a lot tougher in the 1960s and 70s when the world was less mechanized, but even with the technological advancements, landscaping was still taking its toll on the ageing brothers.

Few tasks extruded more sore muscles from the workers than the art of forming root balls on the larger nursery trees so they could be transplanted. First, a circular trench had to be hand dug around the trunk to incorporate most of the roots within a great clump of earth. Two or three men would be in the trench at one time. Sweat dripped off every brow as sharpened spades sliced through roots and metal clanged against stone and soil. When in his prime, no one could dig faster than Jim. The trick was to dig down as far as the roots go then undercut at an increasing angle. Before cutting all the way through, the root ball had to be wrapped with burlap. Digging continued underneath the ball, and finally cutting through the anchor root would free the wad.

The tree had to be carefully leaned over so the rolled burlap could be placed under the root ball. Then the tree was leaned in the opposite direction so that the burlap could be pulled through then the ball was tied up with twine. Getting the whole damn thing out of the hole took several men heaving or rolling. Often Jim could use a tractor at this point but not in a nursery where the trees were close together. All in all, it's one hell of a job, but something that just had to be done. In the later years, modern specialized equipment and more efficient techniques helped reduce a lot of the grunt work, but no way around it, landscaping still involved a lot of intense physical labour.

By the 2010s, landscaping was a smaller part of the business than it had been. Getting completely out of it was out of the question, however. With the intense competition in the garden supply business, providing residential landscape design, planting, and installation services gave Kamstra an edge over the grocery and department store garden centres. The days of the industrial-sized sodding and planting contracts, however, were over.

CHAPTER 19

Well Water with Fizz

A modern household needs a water supply. In the country, this generally comes from a well. Although the original farm had a well, it was not sufficiently deep to provide enough of the essential liquid for both the new house and garden centre. Jim contracted a well driller who bored down over 60 metres within the existing well and installed a submersible pump. There was something peculiar about the water, though. When a tap was opened to fill a glass, the water initially came out white, filled with the tiniest of air bubbles, almost like soda water.

The bubbles would fizz to the surface starting at the bottom and after about 15 seconds the water became crystal clear. It was odourless and tasted good as water should. Jim had a water sample tested for bacteria and the results came back fine. The bubbles were a result of air that was trapped in the bedrock and dissolved within the groundwater. Although it seemed strange at first, everyone in the family soon got used to this naturally carbonated water and thought nothing of it.

Jim expected that the air would eventually dissipate from the well and then they would then have non-fizzy water like normal people. Instead, the water bubbles intensified, but ever so gradually. A few years later when a faucet was turned it would sputter out a blast of air before any water came gushing out. The long-necked kitchen tap came alive, bucking up and down as it coughed out a mixture of liquid and gas. Corry was getting annoyed when working at the kitchen sink. When a toilet was flushed, the tank would gurgle uncontrollably.

"There might be methane or natural gas in the bedrock at the bottom the well," one visitor to the house suggested.

But this was not a part of the province known to contain natural gas deposits. Jim turned on the kitchen tap then lit a match as it started sputtering. A soft blue flame danced around the sink.

"Holy smokes this stuff is flammable!"

Methane is a colourless, odourless, and highly flammable gas that is not toxic in itself. It forms through the natural decomposition of organic materials and can be trapped underground for millions of years. Thus far no-one had experienced any ill-effects, so the family continued to use and even drink the well water just as they always had.

Some months later, Jim and Corry had invited a middle-aged couple visiting from Holland over for dinner. The savoury meal had been devoured and they were enjoying a leisurely dessert when the lights cut out and the room went dark.

"Electricity goes out at the most inopportune moments," said Corry. "Not to worry, we will just pull out some candles and we can continue."

Candles were lit, casting off their warm light and long shadows. The visitor excused herself to use the small washroom near the entranceway. A small, scented candle was glowing in there too. She did what she needed to, washed her hands, flushed the toilet, then casually walked back to the kitchen, closing the door behind her.

Thirty seconds later, "KA-BOOM!"

The bathroom door blew clear off the hinges and tore out the moulding. Smoke poured out into the hallway and kitchen. Everyone looked at each other in disbelief. Jim rushed over to see what happened. The wallpaper was charred, burned off in seconds with the explosion. When the toilet was flushed, the natural gases from the water flowed into the room, then was instantly ignited by the flame on the candle, with unfathomable force. Fortunately, she did not linger in the washroom after pushing down on the flush handle.

CHAPTER 20

Students from the Netherlands

Kamstra Landscaping has employed hundreds of workers over the years. Some stayed for years, others lasted days. Jim expected serious labour out of anyone he hired. Students need to find their first job which can be a challenge since they have no experience. Many times, a customer or friend would ask him if he could give their son a summer job. Jim frowned upon these requests for he knew that if the youth was lazy, he would have to be fired resulting in the possible loss of a customer or friend. A student who applied on his own showed more integrity and therefore a better chance that he would be a good worker. Sometimes Jim gave in, hired the lad, and sometimes it worked out well.

One time, Jim received a letter from Waringa, an old friend from the Netherlands, who explained that his son studied horticulture and needed practise abroad as a requirement for graduation. Could he spend a work term with Kamstra in Canada? Jim agreed, after all, it was for an old friend. Twenty-year-old Rob Waringa came to live and work with the Kamstras for six months in 1981. Rob was likeable and a moderately good worker, but he was quiet, often keeping to himself and as a result, didn't grow on Jim and Corry.

On one of Jim and Corry's trips to the Netherlands, they stopped in to check out the highly acclaimed horticultural college at Boskoop, as a possible place for one of their sons to study. That never happened but leaving his name and address with the college, resulted in getting written requests from students who wanted to work with Kamstra's since the program required students to work for one term in another country. Jim was willing to help out some of these fledgling horticulturalists. As well as assuring employment, Kamstra also had to provide accommodation in their home. That was fine since the house had plenty of room now that the sons had all moved out.

Over the course of several years a few young male students flew across to spend a growing season. One student per summer was long enough for Jim and Corry to put up with a stranger within their home. One summer they accepted applications from two 20-year-old women: Ineke and Jeanette. This arrangement worked amicably. Ineke and Jeanette were hardworking on the job and helpful around the house. The two blonde girls were so much more fun than any of the preceding male students. Corry loved having a couple of animated, Dutch-speaking young women around, like the daughters she never had. Jim had hopes that one of them might pair up with Ted but that never happened. The girls only came for one summer, but it was a memorable one. Ineke never forgot Kamstra's hospitality. Although she never came back to Canada, she maintained contact with Corry for decades afterward.

Corry's dearest childhood friend, Annie Pol, came for a visit to Canada in 1985 accompanied by her husband and two sons. The Pol family spent an afternoon and dinner with Jim and Corry; their younger 13-year-old son, Alex, was fascinated by Jim almost from the moment he laid eyes on him. Jim was a dynamo who did it all. He flew airplanes, had a pond with fish and he told such engrossing stories. Canada just struck the youngster as a fun place to be. Three years later Alex, now 16, wrote a letter to Jim asking if he could come to stay and work for the summer. How could Jim refuse?

    Alex was a lively, lanky boy with dark hair and intense blue eyes who was ready to try almost anything. Perhaps Jim saw something of himself in the lad for the two seemed to share a kind of bond. Sometimes after a hard day of work, Jim would take him for a short flight or out fishing on a weekend. Alex was willing to toil with whatever job was given to him. Even as a teenager Alex accomplished more in a day than some of the seasoned employees. He flew back home in late August but would return to work at Kamstra Landscaping for three more summers.

    In 1991 Alex stayed for more than a year and he lived in the house with Jim and Corry for most of this period. Jim was like a father to him and Alex's keen interest in fishing made them closer as none of his sons shared it. Nevertheless, when on the job, Jim did not show Alex any favouritism. He was expected to work as hard or harder than any other worker. The tall youth did not come as a landed immigrant or a seasonal worker, however, consequently, he did not have the legal papers to work in Canada. When work slowed in the late autumn, fearing suspicion from government authorities, Jim requested that Alex move out. Alex moved in with Harry for a while but then returned to Holland in frustration.

Alex Pol and Jim in 1989.

Alex decided to study landscape architecture; when he graduated, he found a job as a landscape architect for a firm in his native homeland and was working his way up to a successful career. Something about Canada still pulled at his consciousness, however. He just could not let it go. In 2004 at the age of 34, Alex took the steps to finally emigrate. Jim helped with the application forms through Immigration Canada and assured authorities that Alex would be hired on full time in the responsible role as a foreman at Kamstra Landscaping. He could be legally employed at last. Not so young anymore and after a twelve-year break from physical labour, Alex found the work more strenuous than he remembered. He knew that he could get through it for he had the same dogged determination as Jim.

More mature now, Alex became acutely aware of the two different sides of Jim. At leisure or on the offseason, Jim and Alex would fish, share drinks, sing Dutch songs, discuss their philosophies of life, and confide in each other. When Jim was focused on the work it was a different story. The job had to be completed as efficiently as possible, and when there were screw-ups…watch out! Like Jim, Alex was a man of high ambition. He would not be content to be a mere foreman forever, and he questioned if he would ever be able to become anything more within Kamstra Landscaping.

Alex learned of a small competing landscape business that had come up for sale. That sounded appealing; he could buy it and become his own boss. But he couldn't just leave Jim after all he had done for him. Alex approached Jim to let him know of this opportunity, keeping an open mind to discuss options. Jim dearly wanted Alex to stay. He was open to a better arrangement for Alex, if not a full partnership, then maybe he could oversee the landscaping sector. Jim assured Alex that he would discuss it with his business partners, Harry and Ted.

In the end no suitable arrangement could be agreed upon. Kamstra Landscaping was a family business, and Alex was not family. Alex decided to leave. Jim was deeply disappointed, but he could relate to the aspirations of the younger man. Albert Rundle must have felt the same when Jim gave his notice to leave Rundle Garden Centre so many years before.

Alex recalled one of the last days that he and Jim worked together. Just the two of them were pruning Christmas trees at Kamstra's tree farm. The decision had been made which created a tenseness in the air. Neither said much. Each man with a pair of clippers in hand walked among the rows of spruce frantically snipping off boughs to give shape to the little trees.

A light drizzle began to fall, yet the clippers kept clipping. The drops fell harder and harder, eventually turning into a heavy downpour. Two stubborn Dutchmen, totally drenched, kept snipping away, as one would not show his weakness to the other. Who would call it quits first? Neither did; they continued working in the rain until the job was done.

When they hopped in the truck, Jim said, "Alex you are one hell of a worker! I am going to miss you."

Soon thereafter Alex left Kamstra Landscaping and although he did not purchase the small firm, he did eventually start his own successful landscape enterprise, putting the same kind of effort into it as Jim did.

CHAPTER 21

Social and Service Clubs

Jim loved his adopted country of Canada and proudly called himself a Canadian. Nevertheless, he also maintained a fierce pride in his Dutch heritage, since it was the land that made him who he was. Many of his friends, as well as business associates, were immigrants from Holland, like himself. It could be expected that ties to the homeland were strong, particularly in the first years after immigration since there was so much nostalgia, with a common language, music, and ethnic food, not to mention a little bit of homesickness.

An energetic group of naturalized young Dutch people came together in 1958 with the intent of forming an ethnic social club for Dutch immigrants. They would call it the Oshawa Dutch Club. Heck, immigrants from other European lands had created their own clubs in the city: Germans, Italians, Ukrainians, and Polish. Jim was one of the charter members along with Bill Andringa, Cor der Hertog, John Kessler, Sebastian Van der Laan, Jake Vos, and Mary Westerdyk, who would become the executive. Each charter member was tasked with enrolling ten members who would pay $10 to join, providing enough of a cash base to promote and hold events. A surprising number of couples and young families of Dutch descent resided in the area; many were eager to socialize so the membership grew.

Monthly dances were popular and well attended. Members could come out and relive their youth as they danced to the music that they grew up with on the other side of the ocean. Sometimes a Dutch singing live band with accordion, barrel organ bass, and percussion were brought in but usually a disc jockey would spin records of the music that the audience desired. Jim put his talents to good use, as one of the chief organizers. He would secure a liquor license so they could sell booze, which helped make the dances profitable or at least break even. He always jumped in to help with setup, cleanup, and other tasks to make sure each event ran smoothly. He also made sure to be part of the fun, indulging in his share of drinks and leading Corry around the dancefloor to many a lively tune.

Oshawa Times newspaper article about Dutch Club dance showing Corry and Jim.

The club also arranged an annual all-day picnic at a public park. Again, it required much organizing by the executive members, catering in food, barbecuing a whole pig on a spit, running games with prizes for the kids, putting up the big tent. Over a hundred people came out to partake in these feasts.

One year the Dutch Club organized a *Sinterklass* parade and party for children in Oshawa. In the Dutch Christmas tradition, on December 5th, the present-bearing *Sinterklass* (St. Nicholas) comes riding in on a white horse followed by his two black slaves known as Black Peters (*Zwarte Piet*), who are actually costumed Dutch youths with painted black faces. Jim rented a white horse from a farmer he knew and hauled it by truck into downtown Oshawa for St. Nicholas to ride. Cor der Hertog filled the role of the present bearing figure, decked in a bishop's cap, red robe, and flowing white beard carrying a long wooden staff coiled at the top. Cor was not accustomed to riding in the first place plus the roads were icy due to an unseasonable cold snap. One of the most memorable parts of the parade was when the horse slipped, nearly throwing him off.

The Dutch Club was more than just a social club, it was also a marketing opportunity for any members who were business owners. Members were more likely to patronize establishments of people they knew of common nationality. The club newsletter offered inexpensive advertising. Jim was able to use the club to good effect; many members became customers. Jim played an organizing role with the club for over a decade.

A new group of members effectively ousted the old executive and changed the direction of club activities in the early 1970s. The former executive including Jim stepped down. He had enjoyed organizing events, the comradery and he made many long-lasting friends, but running the club was a lot of work and he felt that it was time to do something else. Besides, the demands of his own business had greatly increased by this time. He continued on as a passive member, but then in 1979, Jim and Corry were invited to be the Dutch Club's honorary "prince and princess," to represent the Dutch Club at various ethnic events in the city.

'Princess Corry' and 'Prince Jim' representing the Dutch Club.

Despite his new claim to "royalty", Jim felt handicapped when he compared himself to some of his more sophisticated business acquaintances. He felt his limited education and a Dutch accent that he could not disguise might be holding him back. He sought out opportunities for self-improvement, especially where it might help in business. One year he attended the annual convention of the Ontario Nursery Trades Association, of which he was a member. There were booths from various dealers trying to sell equipment, expertise and other supplies to the attending plant growers. Part of the convention entailed a panel of speakers from the plant growing trade who gave presentations on relevant subjects. One of those men stood out among the others, delivering such an eloquent speech, the audience seemed to hang onto his words. Jim was impressed. It wasn't so much the topic but his flawless command of words, and the confidence that he exuded.

If only I could speak like that, he thought.

After the presentation, Jim approached the man with a targeted question: "How can I learn to speak the way that you do?"

"I suggest you start with a Dale Carnegie course," was his helpful reply.

Jim found out that such a program was offered in Toronto, so he signed up. Every Monday night Jim drove into the big city for a three-hour training session. Dale Carnegie did not teach the course himself, for he had died in 1955, but he had developed courses on self-improvement, public speaking, and salesmanship that continued to be taught by his followers for decades after his death. Millions across North America have read his books and participate in this program. The cost was high, but the investment would pay off. Jim listened, learned, and was determined to apply these new skills. The instructor employed tactics to build up enthusiasm and stressed its importance in developing self-confidence.

"Act enthusiastic and you will be enthusiastic!"

Jim got to know some of his classmates. One introduced himself as Carl Brewer and proclaimed, "I like to play a little hockey".

Turns out he was a defenceman for the Toronto Maple Leafs. Ron Ellis, another Maple Leaf player, was also in the class working on becoming a better public speaker. At the course graduation, everyone had to deliver a prepared speech to a hall with an audience of over one hundred. Jim was nervous but remembered the motto. "Act enthusiastic and you will be enthusiastic!" He was voted "most enthusiastic student" in the class.

Eager to practise his new skills and develop them further, he joined Toastmasters. This international organization encourages members to develop confidence through a set program of preparing and delivering speeches that are evaluated and critiqued. Weekly evening meetings at the YWCA building in Oshawa provided another networking opportunity where Jim met new entrepreneurs and developed more business relationships. In addition to the regular speech program, the club ran annual speech contests. Jim decided to enter.

He wrote a passionate speech on a topic of interest to a wide audience and rehearsed it until he had it memorized. Using hand gestures, vocal variety, humour, and a clear progression through his topics, the judges were impressed, putting Jim in first place at the club level. He next presented the same speech at the Area Level where winners from several clubs competed, and didn't he win again? Delivering a more polished version at Division Level, judges gave Jim another first-place finish. At the Toastmasters District Convention in Toronto, winning speakers came to represent their divisions from across the province. Kamstra entertained a thousand unfamiliar faces with his practised witty monologue.

He may have been nervous but that did not show. With his now subtle Dutch accent and dynamic charisma, he finished to tremendous applause. The judges gave him a second-place finish. The first-place winner was Henry Shannon, a well-known traffic announcer from the Toronto radio station CFRB. Henry reported live daily on the air and therefore public speaking was his profession, so hardly a fair competition.

Oshawa Times article about Jim winning Toastmaster speech contest.

After meeting the challenge of speech contests, Jim moved into the role of president of Oshawa Toastmasters for one term. After that experience, Jim decided that he had learned as much as that organization could offer him.

Albert Rundle had urged Jim to attend a meeting of Kiwanis, a different kind of social club. Kiwanis is an international service club, with hundreds of branches in about eighty countries. The organization's altruistic mandate is to support or engage in volunteer humanitarian work at the community level. Albert had been a charter member of the Oshawa chapter known as the Westmount Kiwanis when it formed in 1958. Jim liked the positive attitude of the members, many of who were well-positioned locally, so he joined Westmount in August 1970. The club supported a children's music festival, food banks, food drives for the poor, pleasure drives for those with limited mobility, and arranged specific projects to improve the lives of less privileged members of society.

While Jim believed that helping those less fortunate than himself was a noble goal, the shrewd side of him also saw that Kiwanis provided an excellent business networking opportunity. Many business owners, professionals and some of Oshawa's more affluent citizens were active members. Weekly meetings at the busy YWCA provided many chances to interact and get to know these people. With his forthright but friendly approach, Jim easily met new people. He would build strong long-lasting friendships with several members and it also paid off in securing business contracts.

Jim was never one to sit back and let others do the work. He would complete a job efficiently and effectively whether it was for his business or for the organization. That is just the way he worked. Within a year of joining the Kiwanis Club, he was chair of the agriculture and conservation committee, but he was more of a hands-on guy than a committee leader. With his ready access to trucks, tractors and other equipment, he was often called when large items had to be moved or installed. He helped construct a public observation tower at Oshawa Second Marsh and clean up the garbage out of the Oshawa Creek valley. Even Corry helped; she was in the water pulling out shopping carts, that had been pushed in by irresponsible youth.

Jim took handicapped seniors on Sunday afternoon drives, just to give them an outing since they rarely went anywhere. He cheerfully toured them around the countryside pointing out different types of trees, landscaping jobs that he worked on, properties of people he knew, or he would just make up stories. He was never short of words for this captive audience, and they were suitably entertained.

Perhaps Jim's biggest contribution to Kiwanis was his flair for fundraising. He just knew how to make money. First, he organized bingo nights, but the profits were low for the effort required, and spending long evenings in smoky bingo halls soon lost its appeal. He then approached CEOs of some companies and was able to talk them into donating a high-value item such as a snowmobile or boat. The item would be used as the prize enabling Kiwanis to sell large numbers of raffle tickets at malls.

The annual Kiwanis Christmas tree sale was Jim's legacy. If anyone understood all aspects of this business it was Jim, who still operated a couple of tree lots for Kamstra Landscaping. He also knew that the public was more willing to purchase their trees from a volunteer organization like Boy Scouts than from a commercial retailer. So why not Kiwanis? Jim set up the lot, delivered a truckload of trees, and advised the other members on customer service.

Jim and Harry with trucks loaded with Christmas trees.

"You have got to be a good salesman," he instructed. "Don't let a potential customer leave without selling them a tree."

He made sure the Kiwanis lot was in a different part of town from his lots so the two shops would not be competing. All profits raised from these ventures would fund the club's various humanitarian projects.

In 1985, the Westmount Kiwanis Club was searching for a big fundraiser. Fellow Kiwanian, Andy Koziar, and several others, like Jim, were keen fisherman so they considered organizing a fishing derby. They contacted Reno and Angelo Viola, the brothers who owned Barclays Sporting Goods, a popular hunting and fishing store in Oshawa. The well-known fishermen presented at a Kiwanis meeting, stating a opportunity to start for a bass tournament since there were none in the province. The brothers gave the Kiwanians advice on how to organize it. Andy was willing to be the frontman; he was going to make this happen.

First, he approached the Scugog Township council to see if such an event could be held on nearby Lake Scugog. Seeing how a sudden influx of sportsmen would benefit local businesses, the township was on board and issued the event permit. First organizing, then executing such a tournament was more than the club bargained for: advertising, taking registrations, obtaining prizes, renting beer tents, catering food, erecting barricades, and setting up a fish weighing station were only part of it. Since the tournament would catch & release the fish, they needed special fish holding tanks and transfer sacks.

Jim looked after much of the physical setup since he had Kamstra Landscaping trucks and tools at his disposal. He coordinated many of the other volunteers to divvy up the labour, doing much of it himself. How was it that Jim worked harder and faster than anyone else? Perhaps because his working life was more physical than the others making him more fit. Jim also had this ability to keep track of the multitude of tasks that needed to be done, rarely writing anything down on paper. The fishing public responded well, entry fees were sent in and prior to the date, registration was full.

On tournament day, eighty high-powered boats loaded with tackle roared out from the Port Perry docks at the 7:00 am start, racing out to all corners of the lake where they would drop their lines. Since there were substantial prizes for the biggest and heaviest fish, not to mention fisherman's pride, some participants might consider cheating to win. Perhaps a fisherman had caught "big one" before the tournament and hid it underwater for retrieval today. Jim had his Cessna on floats, parked on the dock for surveillance. Periodically he took it up to buzz around the contestant's boats, to check on their locations and what they were up to.

Other Kiwanians had their turn in the co-pilot seat in the role of spotter. Andy was the first, and it was his first time in a single-engine aircraft.

"Would you like a better look at that boat, Andy?" Jim asked.

"Yes, sure that would help."

Jim put the plane in a sharp bank, tilting the left wing skyward. Andy looked downward, face pressed against the side window, and he could sense his stomach coming up. "Okay enough already!"

Erna Taylor also a novice to flying, reluctantly climbed into the cockpit when it was her turn. She was afraid to look out the window as the plane gained altitude.

"Jim can you fly lower, please? I would feel safer," she cried out.

"Actually, Erna, the higher we go the safer it is because if the engine conks out, we would glide further and have a better chance of reaching a good place to land."

Erna did not say another word.

No suspicious behaviour was detected among the fishing boats. The tournament concluded with all contestants back at the landing for award presentations and prizes. Barclay's Sporting Goods had donated a brand new 20-horsepower Mercury outboard motor, a great enticement for selling lottery tickets. When the winning number was announced, the ticket holder was Angelo Viola, owner of Barclays! What was the chance of that happening? He certainly did not need it. Jim offered Angelo $1000 for the outboard which he accepted. Half an hour later another participant offered Jim $200 more, so Jim just sold it on the spot. Always happy to make a buck whether he needed it or not.

The tournament was hugely successful, granting huge bragging rights for the catcher of the biggest bass. Running the event required substantial effort by about twenty-five volunteers, but it was a heck of a good time and a substantial fundraiser for the club. Kiwanis organized bass fishing tournaments for another two years, one on Lake Dalrymple and another on Pigeon Lake. Bass tournaments continued to grow in popularity but from 1988 onward the newly formed Pro Bass Canada coordinated them. These events got too big for Kiwanis to manage.

Jim guided the club as elected president for one term from 2001 to 2002. Kiwanis held an annual summer barbecue for its members and their families. For many years, Steve Kisil invited the group to his spacious backyard in Oshawa, complete with swimming pool. When Steve passed away, Jim and Corry offered up their place. Their sprawling back lawn surrounded by hedges could easily accommodate more than a dozen picnic tables. The neighbours were far enough away that the Kiwanians needn't worry about complaints should anyone get rowdy. No-one wanted to miss it. Jim would end the picnic by igniting a stack of wood to create a grand bonfire and by shooting off fireworks. At the final barbecue in August 2015, Jim was presented with an award acknowledging his 45 years of service to Kiwanis by president, Ted Curl.

Jim is recognized for his 45 years of service to Kiwanis, presented by president Ted Curl in August 2015.

Chapter 22

Meddling in Real Estate

Corry once said that Jim liked making money more than he liked spending it. While landscaping was the business where Jim focused most of his effort, he also kept an eye open for other opportunities where money could be made. Landscaping was a labour-intensive business, which was fine by him. However, Jim knew that there were easier ways of earning greenbacks, and one of them was…land. Land prices go in one direction and that is up. Property value may stagnate for a while, or even drop a little for a spell, but it almost always rebounds and continues to rise. Land purchased today could be sold for more money later without any effort. It just required some cash for purchase, patience and timing, and a certain amount of luck.

Jim purchased a 14-hectare property on the Oak Ridges Moraine near the Mosport Raceway in 1972. It was a rough piece of land with a small rustic cabin. It had been farmed in the past and although the soil was well-drained it was too sandy and dry for growing crops, except for …Christmas trees, which is exactly what Jim had in mind. Conifers had already been planted on part of it, mostly Scots pine and white spruce in tidy rows.

With the help of his sons and workers, he planted many more. The spindly pines and spruce were pruned in midsummer following the spurt of new growth, to form bushy symmetrical trees that customers would eventually set up in their living rooms and decorate with tinsel. The trees had to be cut in the late autumn, trucked to the lots and sold during the brief Christmas shopping rush. That farm supplied Kamstra's for about six years before Jim sold the whole property for a tidy profit.

Over the years, Jim had purchased and cut Christmas trees from the lands owned by several local growers, including from one particularly scenic property owned by Mr. Power, on the fringe of the Ganaraska Forest. By the early 1980s Mr. Power, then in his eighties, could no longer farm it so he put it up for sale. The terrain was truly varied, much of it consisting of dry hilly uplands with a simple farmhouse and wooden cattle barn. It contained a mature hardwood woodlot, a pond, creek, deep organic swamp, conifer plantations, meadows and shrubland. Jim spotted the real estate sign so enquired about it. He deemed the price to be fair, put in an offer, and took possession of the 80-hectare (200 acre) parcel of land.

The Power property became an investment, a source of landscape materials, and a personal recreation area. Jim planted spruce and pine which were pruned and sold as Christmas trees a half dozen years later. There were also wild unpruned balsam firs that could also be harvested for Christmas trees. A bit scraggly perhaps, but balsams were still a novelty tree in those days. The swamp at the west end of the property was underlain with deep organic peat soil. Jim had the trees removed then dredged and trucked out numerous loads to the Kamstra Landscaping yard. The rich black peat was an essential component of Kamstra's triple-mix soil. Two large additional ponds were created in the process.

Power's semi-dilapidated farmhouse was fixed up. Jim and Corry used it like a cottage, a year-round weekend retreat. It became their hideaway, less than forty kilometres from home. When they weren't relaxing there by themselves (which for Jim usually meant engaging in property management of one kind or another), they hosted many social events there: birthday parties, family reunions, Kiwanis picnics, and snowmobile parties. Having friends and relatives come over for the day to enjoy his property gave Jim a sense of fulfillment.

Jim was very generous in this regard, for not only did he share his property, but he would also happily cover all of the expenses for those who came. Maybe he felt that this was a way to share his success with other family members that were not as well off as he. In July 1994, he organized a family reunion for the Kamstra clan, including the extended family of his only first cousin in Canada, Grace Van Dyke. Ben, son of Jim's brother Douwe, brought his family over from Holland for the occasion. Jim rented horses from a nearby stable giving everyone the opportunity for a trail ride.

On a frigid wintery Saturday night (about 1992) Jim and Corry were alone in the little house cleaning up the dishes. They had finished Corry's deliciously prepared dinner and decided to go for a walk on this beautifully clear starlit night. Before stepping outside Jim stuffed as much firewood into the woodstove as he could to ensure that the house would be toasty upon their return. They took a stroll to the south end of their property, trotting through the crisp snow, and then looped back to return. An eerie glow was visible in the sky to the north, was that the Aurora borealis? No, it was too red. They came over the hill and to their horror saw flames spilling over the side of the roof. The house was on fire! Sirens range out in the distance, getting closer and closer. Fire trucks soon arrived in their laneway. Rubber suited men wearing helmets pulled out hoses then turned on the water to douse the flames, soaking the little house.

The fire crackled, then hissed, as white steam rose from the structure. The fire was out but the damage extensive. Water froze quickly forming icicles on the eaves and with the structure cooled, thick coats of ice covered everything. Jim and Corry watched the whole ordeal in horror but thanked the firemen before heading home to Oshawa for a sleepless night.

They returned in the morning to assess the damage. What didn't burn had been severely damaged by the water. Not much of the house was salvageable. The frame and some walls were still largely intact, so Jim had the house rebuilt in the spring. When finished, the new house had much the same layout but was more structurally sound. Blue plastic siding replaced the former red false-brick tarpaper and a spacious backroom with large windows was added. Jim and Corry continued to enjoy the property for another few years. In 1997, Ted bought the "Power Property" from dad. The refurbished house would become his home for twenty years before he knocked it down and built a modern house in the same location.

House on the Power property before the fire. *Same house upgraded after the fire.*

Jim bought another 20-acre farm property with a rickety old house on Taunton Road, several kilometres east of Kamstra Landscaping in 1975. He planted out much of the land to trees and shrubs that were used as nursery stock on landscape jobs. With the help of his workers, he fixed up the house to make it liveable, then rented it out. Leasing a house did not always work out so well, however. One tenant, constantly behind with the monthly rent, moved out with several months' rent due, leaving a great quantity of garbage behind.

In another case, a tenant lived in the house for a few years, then moved out but continued to promptly mail in their monthly installments for months afterwards. Jim went over to investigate the condition of the property and discovered that this tenant ran a business pumping waste fuel oil out of old storage tanks. When Jim removed the cover from the well, he found out where the jerk had been dumping the toxic substance. The aroma of stale diesel oil rose out of a well full of a rainbow-streaked viscous liquid. There was no telling how much of the surrounding groundwater table was contaminated and by this time the tenant's whereabouts could not be traced.

It was now Jim's responsibility to pump out and properly dispose of the waste oil. A new well had to be drilled on the opposite side of the property. The house was renovated, largely by Harry so that he could move in. Harry lived there with his young family until 1993.

That property lay at a strategic location where a major interchange would be constructed. It would become the onramp of Taunton Road onto the new toll Highway 418 that would link to Highway 407. The land was expropriated for the assessed market price by the Ontario Ministry of Transportation in 2009 and the house was demolished. Construction did not begin until eight years later. The fully operable interchange opened to traffic early in 2018.

In the early 1990s, Jim purchased a 25-hectare property south of Lindsay consisting entirely of wetland, a mixed swamp of cedar, spruce, and balsam fir. The swamp was underlain with deep organic soils that had accumulated over thousands of years through the slow processes of succession, growth, death, and decomposition. Jim wanted this property to extract the rich black peat since he had excavated what he could from the Power property and needed a new supply.

Over the years Jim had purchased a dozen different properties for purely speculative, or in some cases, in addition to other utilitarian purposes. Some he only held for a couple of years, before selling for a profit. He did particularly well in one case where one of his developer contacts offered to purchase a scenic property for nearly twice the price that Jim had paid, only two years earlier. In another case, Jim checked out a parcel that he thought was over priced. He offered the farmer who was selling it a substantially lower figure than the asking price. The farmer initially scoffed at the offer but then contacted Jim several months later to say he would accept it.

CHAPTER 23

The Sky Beckons

Since he was a boy Jim had a fascination with airplanes. During World War II in the Netherlands, he would marvel at the winged mechanical wonders soaring above him. With the help of a book which identified plane silhouettes, he could tell the various aircraft that roared overhead, and whether they were German, British or American. What was it like to be in the cockpit of one of those he wondered? Would he ever be able to fly himself?

Decades later in a peaceful faraway place with some level of affluence, Jim was able to make that dream a reality. In the winter of 1968, he enrolled in a pilot training course at the Oshawa Municipal Airport. He started with weekly night school to learn about flight theory, regulations and the practical aspects of flying. More exciting was flight training in a real aircraft. Imagine Jim's delight the first time that he put his hands on the controls, "look at me, I am flying"!

First, he had to complete a series of one-hour lessons in a Cessna 150 with the instructor, Hal Wannamaker, beside him in the co-pilot seat. The flight panel with all its gauges looked confusing at first but the eager student soon became intimately familiar with their functions: altimetre, airspeed indicator, turn indicator, artificial horizon, directional gyro, and fuel gauge.

On February 7, 1969. Hal stepped out of the cockpit and said, "okay Jimmy you are ready to make your first solo".

Jim taxied the plane to the end of the runway, then stopped, spun it around, and ran the engine at full throttle from a standstill according to standard procedure. He radioed the control tower for permission to take off. Permission granted, he put the flaps down, pushed the throttle in all the way and felt the force push him back into the seat. The plane accelerated down the runway, wheels gently lifting off the tarmac. He was airborne and rising. True exhilaration, freedom. The Cessna made a wide arc circling the airport, then descended onto the opposite side of the same runway. It was only ten minutes in the air, but it is a milestone for every new pilot, like a baby taking its first step. The plane landed with a bounce, a little awkward but successful. Hal smiled broadly as he watched from the tarmac.

A few weeks later Jim passed both his written and flight tests and acquired his private pilot's licence. His boyhood dream had come true. He would take to the sky at every opportunity.

As a fully-fledged pilot, he was eligible to join the Oshawa Flying Club, to rub shoulders with former World War II pilots as well as others with a passion about aircraft. They had meetings with guest speakers where they discussed aeronautics, new regulations, and shared flying stories. The club also provided a social forum as most pilots are the kind of people who like to party. On many a Friday night, members with their partners would show up at the "420 Wing," a former military barrack converted into a hall near the Oshawa airport. Private pilots told each other tall tales of flying adventures as others listened and the liquor flowed freely.

After one such evening, Jim and Corry invited some of the partially inebriated gang over to their house to continue socializing. Among others, Hal showed up with his new girlfriend, Cathy. Corry put on a pot of coffee to help patrons sober up a bit, then poured a cup to anyone who wanted one. Their uninhibited friend Jake was making eyes at Cathy. He came over to sit beside her and began chatting, putting one hand on her shoulder. Hal thought this a little too forward for his liking. He approached Jake with a full cup of coffee in his hand, then without warning, poured it all on the man's lap.

"Ow, ow, ow!" Jake yelled as he jumped up, steam coming off the crotch of his pants.

Corry was livid. "That's it, I don't tolerate this kind of thing in my house, get out Hal, now!"

"Now Coorrrry," Hal slurred.

"No, out, right now!"

Jim led Hal to the door, pushing him out with Cathy following. Other guests could see that the party was breaking up so soon left.

Hal did not leave, however. He kept ringing the doorbell wanting to come back in for more drinks.

Jim stuck his head out the door. "Get lost, Hal, go home." Then he slammed the door in his face.

Hal kept pushing the doorbell and banging on the door. "Come on, Jimmy."

Jim went to the den and pulled a shotgun out of the closet and stuck a shell in the barrel. He went upstairs to the front bedroom that was shared by Harry and Ted. The boys were awake from the commotion but didn't know what to think when they saw their father come in with a rifle in his hand. Jim opened the window and pointed the barrel out.

"Get going Hal or I'm going to shoot."

"Don't be like that, Jimmy," Hal whined.

Jim squeezed the trigger and the shotgun blasted, filling the room with noise and the aroma of burning gunpowder. He had aimed into the sky just to scare them. Now terrified, Hal and Cathy darted straight for their car and drove off as fast as they could.

While flying would continue to bring Jim exhilarating fun and comradery with fellow enthusiasts, it would also be a source of drama with new experiences, unexpected locales, and even close calls, where mere seconds can be the difference between life and death.

In December of 1970, Jim purchased his first aircraft, CF-JFU, a tail dragging Piper Cub for only $2200. The Cub was a 65 horsepower, two-seater, lightweight, fabric covered plane with simple controls that was easy to handle. It could take off and land in a short distance, and

Jim with the Piper Cub CF-JFU on Lake Temagami.

it could be put on skis in the winter. He first kept the plane tied down on a grassy airstrip at Charley Gabouri's farm south of Courtice for a nominal fee. Half a dozen other planes parked there as well. When Jim could spare a couple of hours he would drive out to the airstrip and take the Cub up for a flight. Often not flying far, just to get experience and soar through the air like a noisy bird. Frequently he would take someone with him in the "shotgun" seat, whoever was willing to go. Corry, James, Harry, Ted, Paul, a friend, sometimes even one of his employees would be offered a free view of the world from above.

Jim had to swing the prop by hand to start the engine of the little plane. It was not a new machine, built about thirty years previous, and it had no onboard starter unlike the Cessna that he learned on. First, he had to turn on the magnetos, prime the throttle a couple of times, leaving it partway out. Then Jim walked to the front, faced the machine and grabbed onto the left blade of the two-pronged propeller. With two hands he pulled down with all his might, then quickly stepped back to be clear of the rotating prop. Usually, the engine coughed on the first attempt. So, he would have to give it another pull or two. Once it caught, the motor chugged for a few seconds, then sped up with increasing noise: time to climb into the cockpit and get the bird airborne.

On a fateful day in November 1971 Jim and son Harry, went for a flight to check out a Christmas tree plantation from above. The flight had been delightful but when they returned, a brisk wind had picked up. The yellow cub descended, making its approach to land when a sudden crosswind destabilized the craft, wings tossing back and forth. Jim pulled up on the joystick, regained altitude, then circled around for a second attempt. Fighting the gusty conditions, Jim was concentrating on keeping the wings level as they were dropping. He did not see the tall wooden pole near the edge of Charley's narrow runway.

The edge of the wing just struck it, sending the plane in a spinning tizzy and flipping it over onto its back. The engine sputtered then conked out. Jim and Harry, still buckled in, were hanging upside down. Harry blacked out momentarily, then gained consciousness in the strange predicament. A loud hiss came from the engine.

"We gotta get out quick! It might catch fire."

Jim released his belt buckle, then Harry's and they slumped down to the ceiling. The door flopped open and out they stepped. Both had a few scratches, but neither was seriously hurt. The plane was quite damaged, however, with a kinked wing and some busted fuselage. It would not be able to fly in that condition.

Fixing the injured plane became a winter project. With help from his metal-working friend, Arnold Paashuis, and brother-in-law, Paul, he dismantled the wings, then loaded the pieces onto a Kamstra Landscaping flatbed truck. They drove it to the airplane repair hangar at King City Airport. The three amigos made daily forays to King City to straighten struts, reapply fuselage and paint the unfortunate Cub until it looked good as new. Technicians and aeronautical experts had to complete the finer details and the machine had to be certified for airworthiness. Once repaired the plane was sold.

It was not long before a second flying machine was in his hands. Jim liked the first Piper Cub so much that be bought another, with the official registration CF-SVA. He constructed a lean-to overhang on the side of the barn at his Taunton Road property keeping the plane very close to home. He could take off from the backyard. A slightly down-sloping grass strip allowed him to take off to the north from his backfield. Jim could slip out for a quick flight when he took a break from work, and in winter there wasn't much work to do. The disadvantage was that the narrow runway was not exactly level, and if the wind was not in a favourable direction, takeoff was precarious or had to be postponed.

One never knew what could be on the rough runway. Jim and Corry had just landed from a short flight and were taxiing CF-SVA back towards the barn. Hector, Harry's Labrador retriever, ran excitedly towards the moving plane. Jim saw the dog coming, but it was too late. They heard a loud "whump!" above the engine's roar, then a black streak raced away across the field and out of sight.

Jim tied down the plane then went into the house. A little later one of the neighbours was on the phone. "Your dog is over here. It has a terrible open gash across its back."

Jim and James drove over immediately to pick up the unfortunate pooch and take her to the veterinarian. Hector had been struck in the middle of her back by the rotating propeller, ripping out a fist sized piece of black fur. Fortunately, the cut did not go deep into the muscle tissue. The vet was able to pull together the animal's skin to stitch up the wound. Hector healed and lived on for years but lost her youthful vigour that day.

Jim, Harry and dog Hector with a Piper Cub at back field of the Kamstra Landscaping property.

When Jim's father, Bauke, visited Canada in 1973, Jim treated him to a flight, taking off from the backfield and over a good stretch of countryside. Bauke was thrilled, and not a bit frightened. At age 71, it was his first time in a small plane. He could see the fields, the layout of roads and houses, the whole landscape: what a view! Bauke returned home soon thereafter and proudly bragged to his friends how his son had flown him all over Canada. Living his entire life in a small country Bauke could not comprehend the vastness of this one.

Sometimes Jim and Paul would make short trips flying side by side in their separate aircraft. Paul owned a blue and white Citabria and Jim his faithful yellow Piper Cub. In winter the planes were put on skis giving them the ability to land on frozen lakes or open snowy fields. One wintery weekend the two flew their planes to Paul's cottage on Lake Temagami.

Next day the adventurers decided to fly to another nearby lake. Shortly after both planes took off, Paul peered through the windshield and noticed that one of the skis on Jim's plane was encased in a chunk of snow and hung down at a steep angle. The ski must have snagged this icy chunk before getting airborne. The plane would not be able to safely land in that condition. Paul radioed Jim to tell of the situation he was not aware of. Jim tried to dislodge the chunk by tilting the flying craft side to side. Then he pulled up to a steep climb, followed by a nosedive. The ice chunk fell off and the ski sprung back into place.

Phew!

In 1977 Jim purchased a Maule aircraft (CF-WKL), another high winged tail dragger with a slow stall speed. It had more power and was a four-seater, allowing more than one extra passenger. With Corry as his co-pilot, he propellered the Maule to Florida in the winter, and the Maritimes in summer. He had made over seventy flights in that beast in one year; he just loved the way it performed. Every once in a while, however, even a smooth-running engine can have a hiccup at an inopportune moment.

On an idyllic September weekend in 1978, Jim and Corry had plans to fly to Mackinac Island, located in the Strait of Mackinac between Lakes Huron and Michigan. James tagged along and also invited his high school buddy, Bob Beckel. The pleasant five-hour flight took them over the Bruce Peninsula and across the great Lake Huron. Mackinac Island was a historic resort town exquisitely maintained in the setting of the late 1800s. Motorized vehicles were not allowed (except planes at the airstrip), so horse carriages, bicycles, and foot were the only ways to get around.

Mackinac's most prominent landmark was the Victoria Grand Hotel, where they roomed for the night. Later the next day on the way back to Oshawa, Jim landed them on a huge turfgrass sod field beside the Nottawasaga Inn, near Alliston, Ontario. The inn was known for its fine restaurant and it was supper time. Although not an official airfield, some private aircraft landed and took off from that wide-open stretch of mowed grass to visit the Inn or dine in the restaurant.

After a satisfying meal, the four boarded the Maule for the final leg of the flight. The plane taxied to the south end of the sod field, turned to face north then prepared for takeoff. Jim pushed in the throttle to give maximum power as he always did on takeoff. The plane lurched forward and began to move, slowly gaining speed across the open field. Without warning, the motor started chugging and the craft was bouncing erratically. The engine was not getting its usual full power, seeming like it did not want to take off. At last, the engine kicked in to run smoothly and gained enough momentum to get airborne. The wheels lifted off the grass, they were going up. A row of steel towers and high-tension transmission lines stretched across the sod field in front of them, right in the planes path. Jim eased off on the throttle to drop below the lowest power line, wheels touching back on the ground. Once clear, Jim gave full throttle. Not much sod field left, but plane was moving too fast to stop now. The Maule airborne again, taking off, climbing.

The very tops of tall poplars at end of the sod field slapped hard against the wings, breaking the ascent. The plane was coming down: it glided over a row of houses, above Highway 89, then towards a plowed field on the north side of the highway. Jim fought the steering column to keep the plane level. Another set of transmission lines crossed that field. The plane made over it them then crash-landed into the dirt. Remarkably the aircraft stayed upright as the loose earth exploded around it as the landing gear collapsed. The nearly deafening engine had stopped dead, all was suddenly quiet.

Jim must have smacked his head on the windshield for blood was oozing out of his forehead. "I'm okay," he said.

Then Corry cried out, "My back, my back, I don't know if I can move!"

The two young men in the back seat, strapped in by a single shared seatbelt, were unscathed. Corry remained seated in position,

Newspaper article in the Cookstown Reporter about the plane crash.

while the other three climbed out of the wreckage. A crowd of people had assembled in the field some to try help, others to gawk. Passing cars on Highway 89 must have witnessed the great bird falling out of the sky.

An ambulance arrived and medical first responders carefully extracted Corry from the dysfunctional Maule. Fearing spinal injury, the attendants strapped Corry to a seat like stretcher, hoisted her into the ambulance, then raced her to the Alliston Hospital. The x-ray revealed that one of her vertebrae had been crushed. She was suddenly two centimetres shorter but remarkably, not paralyzed. After a week in the hospital to recover, she returned home, took it easy for a good while and was able to recover fully.

Surviving two plane crashes could have marked the end of Jim's aeronautical adventures, and it would have for many pilots. Jim was not deterred. Two months after the accident he purchased a Cessna 180 (CF-GNKO), another four-seater with a powerful 235 horsepower engine. And it wasn't long before he planned an awe-inspiring trip across North America.

Jim and Corry along with Paul and Gina signed up for an aerial tour of Mexico in February 1979; they would be flying in Jim's plane. They all boarded the GNKO then flew to Nuevo Laredo on the Rio Grande to meet up with the other 45 participants and twenty-odd private aircraft. Most of the others were farmers from western Canada, hence the group became known as the Flying Farmers. Their charming hosts, Carlos and Margarita, would lead the group through the Spanish speaking land. The line of planes flew across desert, canyons, plateaus, and the rugged Sierras. Apart from viewing the spectacular landscape from above, they landed to take in some famous landmarks on the ground: the stone aqueducts at historic Querétaro, the fishing canoes with their butterfly nets on Lake Patzcuaro, and lavish resorts at Ixtapa.

Like many tourists to Mexico, they indulged in the local food and water, then paid for it with the effects of traveller's diarrhea or "Montezuma's Revenge" as it was known there. Jim and Paul had it bad and took turns running to the bathroom. Corry was afraid to eat or drink anything before boarding the plane. How could they hold their composure when confined to a small cockpit with barely space to move, in the air for hours between landings?

Jim landed the Cessna at the Ixtapa-Zihautanejo airport, then taxied to the terminal. As they were opening the side door, a group of rifle-carrying soldiers in khaki uniforms came running to the plane. What was up? They had seen little evidence of the army in Mexico up to this point.

"Stay in plane," one soldier ordered in broken English.

They did. The other planes in their group also had to comply. Military helicopters circled the airport, then a twin-engine Douglas DC3 came in for a landing. After some time, the soldiers signalled to all that they could exit their planes and enter the airport.

The group later learned that Jose Lopez Portillo, the president of Mexico, was aboard the DC3. The soldiers were carrying out security measures.

The Flying Farmer tour ended at Ixtapa. Later that evening at the steamy resort, Jim made a presentation to Carlos and Margarita on behalf of the group. They were presented with a Mexican landscape sketch with pictures of all of the planes, their registration numbers, and signatures of all participants around the rim. Jim's outgoing nature often got him elected as the spokesperson.

Next morning without the other Flying Farmers or guides, the four climbed into the cockpit, took off then soared northward toward the US border. They could not use VFR instrumentation in Mexico so instead were navigating by aeronautical maps, following valleys and mountainous ridges. The small-scale aeronautical maps they had were hard to read. Corry, the navigator, had to keep track of the landmarks following one to another. Airports, where they could refuel, were far apart, and radio service practically nil. At least the weather was on their side, with bright skies and nearly endless visibility. They lost their bearings for a while, following a valley that was not apparent on the map. Continuing on a northward bearing, Corry eventually recognized the road pattern around a large town, putting them back on course. They landed at the border city of Nuevo Laredo to surrender their papers to the Mexican migracion, then a hop over the Rio Grande to Laredo, Texas. They had covered over 1300 kilometres that day.

The weather took an abrupt change once in the US. Skies turned gray then opened up with a downpour, soaking the normally arid land. They could not fly, so were stranded for days in Laredo. While there, Jim met Al from Pennsylvania who was in the business of exporting Mexican crafts into the US. Having time to kill, Jim and

Corry accompanied Al back into Nuevo Laredo to meet with a broker and check warehouses. Al advised Jim on all the ins and outs about exporting. Throughout the journey, Jim and Corry marvelled at the vast quantity and variety of crafts for sale in markets in Mexico. Textiles, planters, statues, dishes, jewelry of many descriptions; some beautifully designed, others rough or tacky but all made by hand. This chance meeting with Al would be the stimulus for Jim to import Mexican handicrafts into Canada.

Skies cleared the next morning, so the foursome were soon airborne. They made it as far as Tulsa, Oklahoma before being grounded again, this time for a couple of days due to freezing rain. On the final stretch winter weather continued to thwart them. Back in Ontario, snow squalls and limited visibility made for a terrifying flight. They were only 60 kilometres from Oshawa when they hit a wall of snow. Unable to land north of Toronto, Jim turned the plane around, flew below the low ceiling and was able to land safely in Guelph. It had been quite a trip.

In the summer, the Cessna was put on floats and parked at Honey's Landing on Lake Scugog. On some long summer evenings, he would take the floater up for a sunset flight after work. Although not as handy as parking the plane behind the barn, floats offered more landing options in central Ontario where there are vast numbers of open lakes surrounded by dense forest. A plane on floats could take him to distant fishing spots that most other fishermen could never get to.

The far north had a particular appeal, maybe because so few ever went there. With fellow fish and flying aficionado, Paul, he made several trips to Hudson Bay on both the Ontario and Quebec sides. Flying low on one of their excursions along the Quebec coast, they spotted an encampment with several teepees visible along the shore of a large river. They landed on the wide shallow river, then taxied to the shore where they parked and tied up. They probably shouldn't have, but Jim and Paul felt an irresistible urge to investigate this desolate windswept place. They saw no one and heard no human sounds.

Many snowmobiles were scattered about haphazardly. Some were unusable machines with torn windshields and broken tracks, but others appeared to be in working order. They poked their heads into one of the very large canvas teepees. It was well stocked with canned goods, guns, ammunition, spare parts, clothing, and an assortment of items indicating that both men and women stayed here.

This was a native encampment but where were they? The occasional croaking raven overhead was the only sign of life. Was this a winter camp or were the people just out fishing for a few hours?

Jim and Paul had lingered a little too long. The plane's floats now rested on the sandbar; the tide had gone out. The men had no choice but to wait for the water to rise, wondering what the inhabitants would do if they returned seeing them there. Six hours later, still no one, but the water was up so they climbed into the cockpit and got out of there.

Next stop, Moosonee. Fog was forming and thickening over James Bay. Jim feared he would lose visibility altogether, so they made a rough landing on the bay near some small islands. The floats smacked on the pounding waves and water sprayed off the propeller. They taxied around to the lee side of one island where they thought to camp overnight. Jim nosed the plane to shore, careful to steer clear of the many scattered rocks protruding out of the water. They tied up to a couple of the boulders, but Jim felt uneasy.

"If the wind shifts and pushes the plane, the rocks will puncture the floats," Jim worried. "Then we'll never get out of here!"

They noticed that the fog started to lift, visibility was improving. "Let's get out of here," Paul urged.

The trick was getting airborne as the waves on the bay were nearly a half metre high. They faced the plane's nose into the wind, then gave full throttle cutting across through a trough between waves. The plane lagged and rode many crests before it finally lifted off from the resisting saltwater. From there it was clear sailing to Moosonee and then home.

James and his naturalist friend, Bruno Kern, were invited along on one of Jim's Hudson Bay flying adventures in June 1980. Leaving Oshawa, they were in the air most of the day, flying 900 kilometres to Moosonee where they overnighted. The plane sat for some time tied to a dock where one of the aluminum pontoons slowly took on a quantity of water. Jim wasn't sure of the cause, but figured it was likely due to a popped rivet. Each time before takeoff Jim used a hand suction pump to suck the water out of the pontoon's chamber since any extra water added weight which increased fuel consumption.

The following day they continued to fly north following the western shoreline of James Bay. Although mid-June, Hudson Bay gleamed white, completely clogged with ice. The air was barely above freezing, and the land below lacking any trace of green, looked like March. Jim skillfully landed on a widened stretch of the Brant River in the vast Polar Bear Provincial Park, about 15 kilometres inland from the frozen coast. They stepped out onto the brown tundra, into ankle-high shrubs growing on deep sphagnum. The two naturalists hiked out across the spongy terrain to search for longspurs and ptarmigans while Jim stayed near the plane casting out a baited hook into the nearby waters. He easily hooked enough trout from the river for a feast, then built a fire to roast them. After a cool night in the tent, they took off the next morning. Again Jim made sure to pump water from the pontoon minutes before starting the engine and off they flew.

On the way home, Jim landed the Cessna at the seaplane base on Lake St. John to refuel. The stop was to be brief; fill the wing tanks

James and Jim pushing the Cessna ashore on a northern Ontario lake.

with aviation gas, gulp down a coffee, then go. The floatplane taxied to the end of the 3- kilometre-long lake. Jim gave it full throttle. The propeller pulled air as always, but the motion was sluggish. Although water takeoff always takes more power and distance than from tarmac. The pontoons seemed to drag more than usual. Had he remembered to pump out the water? The engine roared and the plane slowly accelerated. It picked up momentum but not fast enough. The darn plane would not break free from the surface. The wooded shoreline was fast approaching. Jim did not cut the engine, trusting that his machine would rise. From the co-pilot seat, James turned to look at his father, seeing sweat streaming down the side of his brow, so complete was his focus.

"Come on, come on, get off the water!" Jim coaxed with gritted teeth.

The floats slowly lifted off and the lumbering aircraft gained just enough altitude to clear the treetops at the end of the lake. Airborne, thank God. No word was spoken, but the memory of a previous ill-fated takeoff hung heavy on both of their minds.

A small aircraft is subject to the whims of weather and Jim did sometimes push it to the limit. In June 1979 Jim and James made a day trip from Oshawa to Pelee Island and back, about 400 kilometres each way. The flight to the far end of Lake Erie was a breeze, mostly clear with light winds. With a rusty pickup truck rented from an islander, the two spent a few hours driving the dusty roads and exploring some of the Pelee Island sites. When it was time to fly back, dark clouds were closing in. The Erie shore provided an obvious landmark to follow for much of the way but then Jim had to cut inland, following a compass heading. The cloud ceiling dropped to a few hundred metres and was so thick that daylight was fading earlier than usual.

It was clear they were not going to make Oshawa. Jim spotted Highway 3 through the fog, then followed it eastward until he recognized the familiar farm of his brother-in-law, Walter Pieterse. The plane descended to make a soft landing in the open sod field across the road (no hydro lines this time). The Pieterse's were quite surprised, as they normally did not have visitors drop in from the sky. Jim and James borrowed their car for the three-hour drive home. When the weather improved, Jim returned the vehicle and flew the plane back to Oshawa.

There would be more aircraft to come and go in Jim's life. Although his first planes were Piper Cubs, the Cessna 172 was probably his favourite. This model was also the most popular private aircraft of all time. He purchased CF-ZKO in 1996 which he flew for about twenty years, by far the longest that any flying machine stayed in his company. The Cessna 172 typically possesses a nose wheel and sits upright. However, before that plane came into his possession, a previous owner had the nose wheel removed and replaced with a tiny rear wheel, converting it into a tail dragger.

All three sons were given the opportunity of learning to fly. Ted joined dad for the occasional short flight when he was younger but rarely once he was a teenager. James loved to go up in his father's plane to view the lay of the land from above and take photographs. He was not so interested in the technical aspects of aviation, however, as he feared that he would get too distracted by the wonders below to make a good pilot. Harry, on the other hand, did have the interest and eventually would become a licenced pilot.

Harry, like his father, had been drawn to planes since childhood. He once even considered becoming an airline pilot, but never lived out that dream. Instead in the late 1990s, Harry purchased a video game program called Microsoft Combat Flight Simulator WWII. With a realistic instrument panel and joystick to operate, this game put Harry in the pilot's seat. The accompanying video screen presented an artificial skyscape, complete with approaching enemy aircraft that had to be shot down. It really felt like flying and the game became an obsession. The constant racket of simulated roaring engines, machine gun fire, and exploding aircraft whenever Harry played, were driving Debbie crazy.

Just a game maybe, but it served as the catalyst that stimulated Harry to take up the real thing. In 2003, he signed up for the required ground school and aerial instruction at Oshawa airport. Jim advised Harry on the intricacies of flying and gave the young man many opportunities to practise. At least one of his sons shared this passion! Two years later Harry passed his flight test. He too had earned his wings.

Harry and Jim didn't always see eye to eye, but they did when in the sky. Harry would rent a plane on occasion to make a recreational flight. Frequently he flew with his father in the Cessna CF-ZKO. Although that plane was like an extension of Jim's body, Harry found it awkward to fly, or at least when landing. He had one close call and after that felt uneasy whenever bringing it back down onto the tarmac. It may have had something to do with the altered tail wheel. Jim decided to sell his beloved plane and look for another that he could better share with his son.

CHAPTER 24

A Mexican Business Venture

While on a trip through various parts of Mexico in February of 1979, Jim and Corry noticed the vast array of handicrafts and folk art that were being produced and for sale wherever they went. The list of items included: ceramics, metalworks, textiles, leather goods, weavings, vases, statues, furniture, masks, sombrero, and other items; the list was almost endless. Items were made for utilitarian and decorative purposes, all collectively known in Mexico as *artesanía*. Mexico is a land of many pre-Hispanic native cultures that persist today, many produced distinctive styles of crafts. Styles ranged from purely indigenous to purely Spanish, but many were a fusion of the two. Towns or regions would specialize in producing certain products in clearly recognizable designs. For example, the state of Puebla was famous for its Talavera pottery, considered to be one of the finest. The workmanship of crafts ranged from exquisite to poor.

At the village of Santa Clara del Cobre which specializes in copperworks, they were able to witness a work being created. A 12-year-old boy held on to a formless slab of copper with tongs. His father and six brothers, arranged in a circle, took turns hammering the blob in synchrony until they had formed a perfectly round flat plate. Nuevo Laredo was a major hub for goods from all across Mexico to enter the United States. Jim, ever open to new business opportunities, contemplated becoming a Mexican craft, the *artesanía*, importer himself.

He looked into the prices of items and investigated how one might import quantities of these goods to Canada. The garden centre was one outlet from where he could sell products but perhaps, he could become a regional importer and distributor. He found out that crafts of all sorts were transported from all parts of Mexico to the northern border town of Nuevo Laredo. Massive warehouses stood on the fringes of the city where wholesalers would purchase their wares then import them by truckloads into the United States.

When Jim had a new idea, he acted upon it quickly. Soon after returning home he decided to give this venture a go. With son, Ted, and foreman, John te Boekhorst, Jim prepared the pickup truck for a long drive to the Mexican border. They drove non-stop, each taking their turn at the wheel when another driver got tired. Washroom breaks, fuel fill-ups, and fast-food meals were their only stops. Thirty-six hours later they pulled into Laredo, Texas at the Rio Grande bridge. They crossed into Nuevo Laredo on the Tamaulipas side, inspected markets and shops and took a tour of Boys Town, the seedy red-light district of cantinas and brothels.

Jim found a customs broker to make the importing arrangements and fill in the complicated paperwork. He then rented a five-ton Rider truck on the Texas side. He mostly chose items that could be saleable in the garden centre such as lawn ornaments, pots, vases, and other ceramics. He also picked out various other curios, such as suits of armour, statues. and "calendars of the sun." Many of the items were inexpensive and of rather poor quality. The price for the fine quality crafts was much higher, and therefore the profit margin for those would be lower. Jim only took a few of those. After a few hours, the truck was tightly packed and stacked to the ceiling with *artesanía*. Now there were three drivers to be shared among two trucks, so they needed to make an overnight stop.

Driving the 3000 kilometres of interstate highway through the central US was uneventful. Attempting to cross into Canada from Buffalo was a different matter. Canadian customs officials were suspicious of a truckload packed full of thousands of supposed Mexican artifacts. That would be an easy place to hide some contraband. All items had to be counted and accounted for.

Knowing this would be a monumental task it occurred to Jim that his niece Celia (Pieterse) Kennedy, who lived only thirty minutes from the border, might be able to assist. He called and she came, willing to help out Uncle Jim. Celia was an English teacher, not an accountant but she was capable, flexible and able to help fill out forms and count items. It took hours of unloading, separating and tallying ceramics with suspicious officials periodically looking over their shoulders. Satisfied that all was in order, the truck with all its wares was allowed in on Canadian turf.

Back at Kamstra Landscaping, the Mexican handicrafts were unloaded. Many items were immediately displayed for sale in the garden centre, but most were stacked and stored in the upper reaches of the barn. Although a lot of the pots and curios were purchased by customers it took years to sell off this inventory. Many of the poorly fabricated pots did not fare well outside in the Canadian winter, they just crumbled apart. Jim tried to wholesale to some stores in Oshawa but with little success—it turned out he was not the only importer of Mexican goods in the area. Several specialty shops in Oshawa also imported and sold a wide range of Mexican wares, mostly of a higher quality than his items. Another business venture under his belt, Jim gave up on the idea of being a largescale importer of *artesanía*.

CHAPTER 25

Hook, Line, and Sinker

As a boy, Jim was entranced by the fish he saw in the ditches and canals around Meppel. His earliest recollection of what inspired his passion for fishing was a "big one" he caught during wartime. That day he spied a large pike lurking motionless on the bottom of the river. Carefully he lowered a line with a hooked minnow on the end, in front of the fish's snout. The unsuspecting beast snapped hard at the bait and was snagged in the mouth. It darted off with the line, nearly breaking free from the boy's grip. Jim grabbed on tight then pulled the line in, hand over hand. He proudly took the fish home for his mother to cook. Any fish that Jim could catch was a welcome addition to the family meal during the war.

A local trick that he learned was to find a section of ditch that was confined between culverts at either end. Jim would block off the culverts with hunks of sod and sticks or whatever debris he could find to cut off escape routes. Then he would drag a rake vigorously along the bottom stirring up the substrate, a process he called *swarte maken* (black making). Panicked fish rose to the surface and Jim would grab them by hand or spear them with a pitchfork. It was relatively easy to get a bag full of fish this way. He caught carp, a type of whitefish, and even eel using this method.

Years, and across an ocean away later, Jim marvelled at the fast-flowing clear water streams in Nova Scotia, a contrast to the sluggish turbid dredged waterways of the Netherlands. Speckled trout and Atlantic salmon swam in these waters. In the Avon River fish moved upstream from the Bay of Fundy with high tide, then returned as the tide went out. When he wasn't working, Jim would walk to the Avon with a fishing pole, making sure to time his fishing when the tide was up. He caught eel here also, but these were the heftier American species. One was as big around as his wrist.

Once moving to Ontario, a land of lakes there were so many opportunities for fishing. Jim recalled his first time out in a rented boat fishing with soon to be brother-in-law Paul Ten Westeneind. It was 1956, one of those lucky days on Rice Lake when the fish seemed to strike the bait every time they lowered a line into the water. Jim and Paul became competitive, who could catch the biggest fish and most fish? They hauled in a fine catch, maybe 20 kilos of perch, sunfish, bass, and even a pickerel: several good meals worth. Walter and Aggie Pieterse with extra mouths to feed would surely appreciate fresh fish. The two fishing buddies put all of their catch in a large plastic bag and presented it to them. Walter left the fish outside in the bag a little too long. When he opened the bag to pull out and clean the fish, he was overwhelmed by a most powerful stench. The fish were fermenting in the sun and all had to be pitched.

When Jim had sons of his own, he would do his best to instill a love for fishing in them; it would be father and son bonding time. On several occasions, Jim took young Jamie and Harry for an afternoon of fishing on nearby Rice Lake or Sturgeon Lake. He rented a wooden boat with a 9-horsepower engine, loaded up the gear with some snacks and drinks, then motored out to promising fishing spots. Their quarry was mostly perch and sunfish, but Jim was more interested in bass or pickerel. Sometimes they still fished at a quiet spot, casting or with lines down in the water.

Jim taking 4-year old Jamie on his first fishing adventure.

Jim's favourite technique though was trolling, the engine put-put-putting along as the boat slowly moved, lines dragging out behind it. Jim had the knack; he could sense a fish when it nibbled on the end of his line. A quick upward jerk of the rod usually hooked his cold-blooded quarry. Excitement reined when suddenly the rod arched over, and the reel sang as a big one pulled out line. Jim played it, reeling it partway in, then letting the fish pull out more line, then reeling it in closer until the fish tired, and he could scoop it out of the water with a net. Occasionally Jamie or Harry caught a fish, but Jim was pulling in most of them.

"If you want to catch a fish, you have to concentrate," Jim directed.

Jamie could not understand how concentrating on the end of the rod, or the baited hook down below would make the fish go for it. Instead, he would daydream, distracted by clusters of whirligigs or water striders that danced across the water's surface near the boat. While the boys enjoyed being out with their father in the boat on a warm afternoon, the fishing part never caught on with them. Jim could not understand it.

Once a year on a mid-spring evening, Jim drove the family to the Lake Ontario shore when the smelt were running. The small fish gathered by the thousands in the shallow waters off the beach to spawn. Jim had a 1 metre square piece of netting extended flat with stiff wire, that hung on a length of string at the end of a pole. No challenge to this kind of fishing. Just let the net lie on the bottom for a few minutes until a small school swam over it then pull up on the pole getting the net out of the water and onto the shore. Everyone surrounded the net, reached in to pick out the flopping silvery fish, then dropping them into a bucket. Other families came out as well for this annual ritual. Some made fires on the beach.

When the buckets were full the family went home. All participated in the cleaning of fish. It was easy, a slice through the belly, then scoop out the entrails with a finger, leaving the fins on and bones in but cutting off the head. Corry would make several meals from this haul. The headless bodies were rolled in flour and salt, then fried in butter until crispy. The family crunched away on the savoury fish devouring all including bones and fins.

On his many travels to sun destinations with Corry, Jim would incorporate a fishing expedition into it whenever he could. On their 1975 Jamaica trip, Jim and Jack Janssen hired a disreputable local to take them and son James out in a little wooden rowboat. The "guide" had no bait, so he raided someone else's fish trap that they passed along the way. He reached in to pull out a medium-sized fish that was cut up. Pieces were inserted on hooks which were at the ends of hand-held lines. No rods or life jackets on this outfit—it was the budget boat. Due to the previous night of drinking at a lively nightclub however, the three tourists were in no shape for an early fishing trip in a rickety boat on the Caribbean Sea. Two of them unloaded their semi-digested breakfasts into the saltwater, then wanted nothing more but to be back on solid ground.

Later in the day, along with their wives, they hired a larger open boat to take them many kilometres out from the Jamaican shore. The boatman was scanning the watery horizon, looking for something as they cruised along the gentle swell. In the distance, more than a dozen great black birds on slender wings circled over what looked like a patch of boiling water. The boatman opened the throttle and raced the craft in that direction. Those were frigatebirds, attracted to a school of tuna jumping at the surface. Perhaps predatory sharks or dolphins had driven the fish to the surface. The boatman knew what to look for alright. Lines were quickly cast into the water, and fish started biting almost immediately. The men reeled in several small tuna and dolphinfish (also known as dorado).

Jim hooked something larger, a real fighter. The others watched Jim strain as the rod bobbed and bowed, then a dark form broke the surface as it neared the boat. It was a king mackerel, certainly the catch of the day if he could bring it in. He kept winding the reel until the sleek metallic body was drawn alongside the boat to be netted. Back at the Golden Beach Hotel, they donated the mackerel and other fish to the kitchen. A great fish dinner was prepared for all of the hotel's patrons that night.

Jim was never shy about approaching local fishermen to see if they would take him out. When he spotted a fisherman, he would strike up a conversation, asking what the man had caught or about the equipment he was using. If he had a good feeling about the dude, then Jim would see if the man could be hired. Then he would try to work out a price, sometimes bartering, or just settling on the original price if it was fair. This worked for him in St. Lucia, Monserrat, Belize, Mexico, the Bahamas and who knows where else. Maybe these local boats did not always meet safety standards, and their onboard equipment could be substandard. Jim knew that it was not possible to have an interesting life without taking a few risks along the way. It was more fun to make his own arrangements.

Corry, Jim and Paul with their catch after being out with a local fisherman in the Bahamas.

In about 1990, Jim started taking more extravagant trips specifically for "catching a big one." Fishing held no spell on Corry, she had no desire to go on those trips. They were boys only anyway.

Great Bear Lake in the North West Territories seemed like as good a place to start as any. As the organizing group leader, Jim needed to sign up ten people for this first trip to go. Not too hard since many fishing buddies could lay down the required cash for such a trip. Paul, Albert Rundle, Arnold Paashuis, and George Westerdyk were among the group that signed up for the fishy adventure. Lake trout were large and abundant and could be seen deep in the crystal-clear waters. Arctic char were even more sought after, as they were well known for their superior tasty flesh.

Paul and Jim formed one team and were out along a river in quest of char. The salmonids were not going for the bait so Jim thought he would try jigging, which sometimes works when conventional casting doesn't. Jigging involves letting the jig, an artificial minnow with a large hook within it, sink to the bottom then moving the rod up and down and side to side to create motion which hopefully attracts a fish, then a quick snap of the wrist to snag it. Jim's hook snagged something alright, but it was not a fish. He was stuck on a submerged rock so yanked the rod violently up and down to get it loose. The hook and line broke free, flung up out of the water, zinged over Jim's head then snagged Paul, right into his ear lobe. Jim pulled out his pliers to delicately snip off the barb to dislodge the hook.

He caught a real big one that day!

Albert Rundle and Jim with a large Lake Trout they caught on Great Bear Lake.

On another day, Jim and Paul, along with their fishing guide were cruising along in an open runabout with a 10-horsepower outboard on Great Bear Lake, about an hour out from the lodge. The motor hummed along seemingly fine, then started sputtering, coughed, and conked out completely. First, they checked the fuel tank. It was fine. The guide fiddled with the tiller, then yanked on the pull cord again and again. Nothing. It would not start.

The others tried it too with no better luck. They checked the gas line, cleaned the spark plug, then yanked the pull cord some more. The blasted machine just was not going to cooperate. Without walkie-talkies or other means of communication, the three of them drifted along through the waves for a couple of hours. Eventually, the staff at Branson's Lodge, where they were staying, realized that a boat was still missing. A rescue crew was sent out to find and retrieve them.

The Queen Charlotte Islands, now known as Haida Gwaii, became Jim's favourite place to fish. A booth at the 2000 Toronto Sportsman Show promoting the wonders of ocean fishing around the Charlottes, off the northwest coast of British Columbia, caught the attention of Jim and Paul.

"Look at that, what do you think?" one asked the other.

A few months later they were on their way to stay at an elegant fishing lodge on the Inside Passage. Catching big fish may have been their excuse for being there, but there was much more to it. The setting, the misty islands, and smell of salty air, not to mention the comradery of being with the like-minded and some good old-fashioned fun. Now in their seventies, Jim and Paul could still act like schoolboys when they were together. They taunted each other. A drink or two, with Crown Royal being the beverage of choice, helped overcome inhibitions they might otherwise have.

Jim, Paul, and another friend, Earl, were on their own in a boat from the lodge. The sky was clear and hot with almost no breeze. While pleasant, such conditions made for poor fishing. They were getting no bites. Bored and in a clowning mood, Paul picked up the flare gun and said, "let's shoot into the air because we are in distress."

He held it out, then yanked on the pull chain, thinking the flare would shoot up. Instead, it fired straight out, right into the boat. A loud crack, sizzle, then crazy sparks ricocheting around the hull, an angry ball of fire skidding across one seat then landing on another, burning a hole through the plastic seat cover.

"Oh-oh!" Paul placed the orange floater jackets over the seats to hide the damage.

Fraser, the lodge owner happened to be standing on the dock as they were returning the boat.

"Hello boys, how did the fishing go?" he called out.

"Not so good," answered Paul. "We were in distress".

The owner hopped in the boat and pushed the floater jackets aside, catching sight of the charred and melted evidence.

"Now you've got me in distress," he replied. "What the hell happened here?"

Fraser was justifiably angry but never charged them for the damage.

The lodge offered a free week stay to the patron who caught the heaviest fish. Jim and Paul had caught a large salmon, but they knew it was a little shy of what was needed. Maybe a little enhancement would do the trick. They stuffed many lead weights down the mouth of the dead fish. Fraser weighed the fish, and indeed Paul's was the heaviest. Something did not seem right because some fish brought in by others were larger. Fraser had the fish gutted exposing their prank and shaking his head. Of course, Jim and Paul were denied the prize. The lodge probably did not care to see them return after those two incidents.

But return Jim did, maybe not to that lodge, but certainly to the waters of Haida Gwaii; and with better catch results on subsequent trips. Several times he stayed on a floating lodge that was stationed well offshore, heading out on smaller fishing boats onto the open sea. The largest fish that Jim and Paul ever caught was a Pacific halibut in deep water. It is not certain which of them hooked the fish but bringing it in took both of them.

Paul and Jim with their impressive Pacific Halibut at Haida Gwaii.

Jim would take the rod, spinning the reel in until he was tired, then pass it to Paul who did the same until he needed a break. Back and forth went the rod, the line coming in closer and closer. A huge dark diamond-shaped form rose from the depths, up to the surface. What a peculiar lop-sided fish, flat and broad with both eyes seemingly pushed onto one side of its face. They called the fish "the hundred pounder" but it was just a little shy weighing in at 98 pounds (about 45 kilos) and about 150 centimetres in length. Many fillets came out of that one.

In 2005 Paul had other commitments (what could be more important than a fishing trip?) so Jim needed another fishing buddy. Fellow Kiwanian, Andy Koziar, could handle a rod as well as anyone, and so made a suitable substitute. After the first adventure, Andy too was taken by the verdant fjords of the West Coast and thus became a regular companion. He would join Jim and Paul whenever he could. Jim had assembled several friends to stay at a remote lodge on the northwest side of Vancouver Island for their 2008 trip. They endured fog, rain, and undulating swells on the open ocean, but the fishing was fantastic.

The week over, all were up early on August 3 with luggage packed. They waited on the dock for the seaplane that would fly them back to Vancouver. They knew it would be a Grumman Goose, an ungainly fat-bodied twin engine that belly-landed on the sea, the same one that flew them there. Someone from the lodge came out to informed them that it would be a couple of hours late. Killing time, Jim, Paul, and Andy wandered into the nearby First Nation village of Kyoquot.

Paul saw a phone booth so he decided to make a quick call to inform his partner, that he would be delayed.

"You're alive!" he heard her say on the other side of the receiver.

"Why shouldn't I be?" Paul asked.

"It's been all over the news: a bush plane crash in the north part of Vancouver Island. I was worried sick that you might be on it."

Paul relayed this news to the others, then they approached the lodge manager. "We just heard that there was a plane crash. Could that be our plane?" Paul asked.

"Yes, it is, but we don't know yet what happened, and we are trying to keep everyone calm," came the reply. A Grumman Goose eventually appeared low overhead, then slid its belly onto the waters of Kyoquot Sound. It was a different plane, a replacement sent to retrieve them.

Later they learned that the original plane, with six loggers on board, had taken off from Port Hardy then headed in their direction. The plane stalled and dipped while attempting a steep climb over a foggy ridge. It could not gain altitude fast enough so crashed into the trees creating a hole in the forest. The emergency locator transmitter in the tail of any plane is programmed to send out signals immediately if a crash occurs. In this case, the device was smashed on impact, rendering it useless. In the mountainous forested interior of Vancouver Island, it took eight hours of searching before the busted Grumman could be located. The pilot and four passengers were killed.

The last trip of the ageing fishing buddies to the West Coast was in the summer of 2014. Paul and Jim were out on the sea with their guide as they had been many times before. Paul had hooked a hefty salmon out on a long length of fishing line. He cranked the reel, bringing the fish partway in, then out went more line. He reeled it in again, out the line went again. It was getting tiring, painful; actually, no longer fun.

"Geez, my shoulder hurts like hell," Paul said. "I can't bring it in!"

He handed his rod over to the fishing guide who skillfully wheeled in the line and the trophy fish.

"That's it! I'm done."

Deep-sea fishing was a young, or at least mid-aged man's game, not for a senior. Paul concluded that he couldn't do the West Coast trips anymore. Jim had his own reason to give up the long fishing trips. Corry was getting frail and should no longer be left home alone for so long.

CHAPTER 26

Accidents Will Happen

Jim up a big tree with a chainsaw showing that he did not always adhere to the highest safety standards.

Jim had more than his share of accidents. Sometimes just sheer bad luck but the cause of several likely stemmed from his overriding philosophy to get things done quickly. His impatience and a general lack of fear meant that Jim neglected to take all the safety precautions. He was usually lucky, getting off scot-free, but sometimes he did not.

A favourite toy, a snowmobile, was fun to drive and could move over snowfields and trails with agility and speed. However, the machine was unstable, easy to capsize and safety gear like helmets and safety goggles were not mandatory in the 1960s and 70s. For his first time on such a machine, Jim tried out a Bolens Hus-ski owned by Albert Rundle. It resembled a metal box on rubber tracks with a light in the front and a handlebar on the back.

The operator and passengers would sit on a separate sleigh, a long-padded seat on skis that was connected to the engine unit with a metal bar. On a sunny Sunday in the late winter of 1967, the family went to Lake Simcoe to try out this unusual vehicle. Jim raced the rumbling machine over the snow-covered lake, with the kids hanging tight on the seat behind. This was fun, what a great winter activity!

A year and a half later Jim decided to purchase a snow machine for himself. The Hus-ski was an awkward design that was hard to steer and had already become obsolete. Instead, he opted for a 12-horsepower Olympic Skidoo, which had skis in front and tracks behind on a single unit. Another year later, he bought a second more powerful 16-horsepower Olympic. On many a snowy winter's day, the family was out on a snowmobile trip perhaps crossing the length of Rice Lake or through the maze of trails in the Ganaraska Forest.

The early snowmobiles were unreliable. Breakdowns were common, especially when machines were running at full throttle for hours across an open lake. They would overheat, sputter, then conk out. It was just part of the activity. Jim was never at a loss on what to do. He would lift the engine cover, check the spark plugs or carburetor, blow into the gas line, or just let it cool off. He was no mechanic, but he could always get the machines going again.

Closer to home, many snowmobile trails were accessible in and around the Farewell Creek valley east of Oshawa. A sled made by his welder friend, Arnold Paashuis, was pulled behind with two kids sitting and one standing behind like a sleigh dog musher. Snowmobile outings often became a social event with other families, especially the Paashuis's and Ten Westeneinds. Sometimes they went on a nocturnal run to Lake Scugog, even on a school night. The 50-kilometre round trip through closed road alignments, forest trails and a frozen lake was an exciting way to spend a frigid night.

On occasion, Jim rode the boys from home to school or picked them up with a snow machine. One boy sat immediately behind the engine in front of Jim and the other two on the long seat behind standing Jim who worked the throttle. Snow would fly as the machine roared into the schoolyard, entering through a gap in the chain-link fence. Other children looked on with envy. No other students came to school that way.

Jim didn't always stick to the trails. In those winters of deep snow, one could zoom through woodlots, farm fields, along hedgerows and snowdrifts that formed along country roads. Jim went out for an evening run with 9-year-old Harry hanging on behind. While crossing a field in the darkness, the front of the snowmobile struck a single strand of electric cattle fence that he did not see. The wire flew up and zinged off the plexiglass windscreen, Jim instinctively turned his head, but the wire still hit him and sliced halfway through his ear. Had he not partially ducked, he could have been partially decapitated. Jim rode the Skidoo back home then Corry drove him to the hospital to get his ear stitched up.

Another time on a frigid night in the winter of 1974 Jim was out with Arnold racing across the snow-covered ice of Lake Scugog at full throttle. They saw no obstructions on the open lake, so it appeared safe. Suddenly an up-thrusted metre-high pressure crack appeared in the headlight beam. Jim's machine hit a wall of jumbled ice blocks. He was thrown from the Skidoo, landing roughly on the ice, breaking his collar bone in the process. Jim was taken to the hospital and bandaged up. He suffered through a long painful winter of limited mobility. The collar bone seemed to be healing well but when x-rayed, his doctor saw that the bones were not in proper alignment. Bones had to be reset, which was very disappointing. More pain and a prolonged period of healing. He just had to be patient, which did not come easily. Nevertheless, Jim made a full recovery.

Snowmobiling was also rough on other members of the family. Harry was riding on the homemade sled being pulled by the Skidoo down a very steep section of trail along the Farewell Creek valley. The sled, attached by a piece of rope, slid alongside the snowmobile that had slowed as it descended down the slope. The sled flipped over with Harry underneath. He let out a scream, so Jim stopped the machine. Harry's arm was broken. On another occasion, Corry was sitting on the seat behind Jim who was throttling the machine up a steep but narrow trail. Another snowmobile was descending the slope at the same time. The two machines came so close that they nicked each other, at the point where Corry's had placed her foot. Metal struck the side of her boot, breaking her ankle. Another trip to the hospital.

Jim riding a snowmobile. It was a lot of fun most of the time.

Once each summer through the 1970s Jim and Corry organized a Saturday afternoon picnic for all of the Kamstra Landscaping staff and their families at the back of the property. Kamstra's employed about a dozen workers so there would usually be twenty to thirty people at the picnics. It was a jovial affair, games for the kids, a swim in the pond, lots of burgers and steaks on the barbeque, pop for the kids, beer and wine for the adults. The highlight was the after-dinner hayride where a tractor slowly pulled a flatbed trailer loaded with bales of hay on a loop through several rural unopened road allowances. People sat on the straw bales, joking, singing, and drinking. Some employees who knew how to operate it, took turns at driving the tractor.

Near the end of the August 1981 picnic, the hayride began as ever. One employee drove the tractor pulling a wagonload of joyous adults and children. Jim was enjoying his beer as he sat along the front edge of the trailer with his legs dangling down. The tractor made a sudden swerve, onto the edge of the ditch. Jim was bumped off, fell to the ground and a wheel of the heavy trailer drove over his shoulder. The ambulance arrived, quickly ending the picnic and delivering Jim to the Oshawa General Hospital. He was bandaged up and remained to recover for several days. This time his shoulder was broken.

Sometimes Kamstra's would truck in loads of firewood to sell it in the garden centre and Jim would use some of it in his own woodstove. Al-

Hayride for Kamstra Landscaping employees at company picnic in 1977. John te Boekhorst is in the foreground.

though the wood was cut, some of it came in very large blocks that had to be split, which was done with the help of a log-splitter connected to the power takeoff (PTO) at the back of the tractor. It was a two-man operation, at least it was if one wanted to be really efficient. One man put the log down on a platform between blade and backstop, the other would pull the lever to engage the hydraulic blade to push through the wood, splitting it.

Jim and a worker were splitting big chunks of wood on an autumn day in the late 1990s. Jim put down a woodblock, the worker pulled the lever, split, Jim put down a block, the worker pulled the lever, split. And so, it went. After a while the repetitive task became mind-numbing, resulting in a momentary lapse of attention. Jim put down a log, either the lever was pulled too soon, or his finger was not placed where it should have been. Jim screamed as intense pain seared through his left index finger. It was severed off in an instant. He was rushed to the hospital with the mangled remains of his finger, but reattachment was not possible. He was left with a stub where his finger had been. He would have to learn to do without it. Even years later Jim would sometimes feel the sensation of a cold fingertip even though there was no finger there.

Mishaps nearly always occur when they are least expected. Jim and Corry were attending a party with a gathering of Dutch acquaintances at a church hall in Courtice. Many of the folks were long-time friends, so they mingled, made small talk, feeling at ease in this crowd. Jim had a clear plastic glass filled with wine in his hand. He took a big sip then suddenly started gagging and hacking. He grabbed his throat. Something hard and sharp was stuck there. It turned out to be a broken piece of a plastic cup. It must have been sitting in the wine that he gulped back. He bent over and tried reaching in with his fingers, but it was too far down. Corry looked in Jim's mouth but could not see anything. Everyone had stopped what they were doing and helplessly stared at Jim bobbing and waving his arms around. Bad as it was, the item did not block his windpipe, at least he could breathe.

Jim was led to the car and Corry quickly drove to the emergency ward at the Bowmanville Hospital. The doctor on call came to help Jim. He looked in Jim's mouth and attempted to remove the object with a metal implement. He was not able to get it out either.

"Well, you can breathe okay, so go home and come back in the morning. We'll get it out then," the doctor instructed.

This was not the help they were looking for, and how was he supposed to sleep in that condition? Before going to bed, Jim went into the bathroom, forced himself to gag and cough continuously. Out popped the pointed piece of plastic. He was able to do what even the doctor could not.

What a relief.

CHAPTER 27

Should Have Left Well Enough Alone

James was looking to buy his first house in the winter of 1992. When he found a property he liked, he would ask his father's advice. Jim would come out, make a cursory investigation of the building's condition, consider the price, and say if he thought it was a good investment. With Jim's blessing, James put down a down payment on a property west of Port Perry that contained a simple three-bedroom, insulbrick-covered bungalow with an unfinished basement. It was sold as a 'power of sale' indicating that the previous owner had defaulted on the mortgage and the property was being sold by the bank that repossessed it. While these properties typically sell for a good price, they come with a 'buyer beware' clause meaning that any issues are the new owner's problem without any recourse. The house seemed to be sound with no obvious flaws.

Jim was over, for a more detailed inspection once the property was James'. James turned on a tap and let it run for a few minutes. The water pump came on automatically to send water through the pipes. Then the pump started to sputter, and water flowing out of the faucet slowed to a trickle. Why was there no pressure? They went outside to check the well. It was an old dug well with a series of cylindrical concrete tiles stacked one on top of the other. They pried the heavy circular concrete top off the well and looked down. The water in the bottom was clear but very shallow. The screened end of intake pipe was sitting in sand. Two of the tiles above the water line had separated leaving a 1 cm gap from where fine sand had seeped out, slowly filling in the well. Sand now occupied about a third of the depth of the well.

Jim knew what had to be done. They dropped a long ladder in, and James climbed down. The quicksand sucked on his boots, threatening to pull him in. James laid out a board to stand on. He filled a plastic bucket with a rope tied to the handle, with the sandy slurry.

Jim pulled up on the rope, dumped out the slop on the ground, then dropped the bucket back into the well. Another bucket filled, up it went. Many buckets later, one tile and then two were completely free from the sand. Water was seeping in, getting deeper with each sand bucket removed. Next Jim entered the well and sealed the gap between the tiles with wet working cement. Problem fixed.

Three years later James married his sweetheart, Lynda May Tomihiro, who then moved into the insulbrick bungalow with him. In March 1999, Lynda gave birth to Nathan Blair, the second grandson to Jim and Corry.

The old well provided them with sufficient clean water until the hot dry summer of 1999. The water table dropped several metres, to the point that the well went completely dry. James hired a water truck to put water in the well but after three days that water seeped away and they were waterless again. With a wife and baby in the house, the water demands were much greater than when James was a bachelor.

Jim came to the rescue once again. He said that he would dig a new well for the fledgling family, but his approach did not exactly follow well drilling protocol. Jim brought in an excavator who dug a huge hole at a new spot beside the bungalow. Being on the Oak Ridges Moraine, the ground on the property consisted entirely of sand. A great mound of sand was forming as the excavator dug deeper. He continued down to 8 metres, extending far into the water table and almost twice as deep as the existing well. Jim had 10 concrete well tiles delivered. The first one was laid perfectly level at the bottom of the pit. Another was fitted on the rim of the lower tile. The base of the tile was backfilled with soil then other tiles were laid on top of each other, continuing up to the surface level.

All seemed fine but when the top tile was placed, it started to lean. The sand bottom of the stacked tiles may not have been sufficiently firm for the whole series had slumped slightly and narrow gaps formed between some of the tiles. Jim was not happy with the prospect of digging the whole thing up again to reset the tiles, he had already devoted days and several workers to this project to help out his son. James suggested that perhaps it was not necessary. They could insert a slightly narrower culvert into the well and then it would not matter if sand silted in around the outside.

This they did with a 6-metre long section of a galvanized and corrugated metal culvert. The well now held sufficient water quantity and the quality seemed good, at least it did in the beginning. Before long, however, the water in the house was emitting a slight but obvious odour and when tested, showed a high coliform count. Somehow the well was being contaminated by surface runoff and a chemical reaction with the metal culvert. All the work on the well was for naught.

A few years later James and Lynda hired a certified contractor to install a deep drilled well. Both the original and second dug wells had to be filled in following municipal regulations. Sometimes it does not pay to circumvent the rules. They are there for a reason.

James and Jim installing the new well. James's 7-month old son Nathan is in the baby carriage.

CHAPTER 28

A Menagerie of Animals

Jim loved animals of many kinds. He appreciated their beauty and strength whether wild or domesticated, but had a pragmatic view of them, and especially liked animals that could be put under his control. It started as a young boy, with the intimate relationship that he had with Tomi, his dog and best friend. Then there were crow and magpie nestlings that he robbed from nests, which he lovingly hand-reared into intelligent responsive pets. Later in Canada with a large place of his own, Jim could raise whatever animals he fancied.

Many dogs would come to know master Jim over the years. One of his first Canadian canines was a German Pointer named Cleopatra. Jim acquired this beast to help him find rabbits which he then hunted with great zeal. This sleek hunting hound could sniff out an almost invisible rabbit hunkered down in a brush pile. The dog would freeze, nose facing in the direction of the quarry, one front paw raised and pointing backwards. Over the years he would have German Shepherds, Border Collies, Labrador Retrievers as well as a few crossbred mutts. Best was to have a dog that would readily come when called, jump up on the box of a pickup truck, and stay there until Jim called it down. Those dogs with a mind of their own that would not come on command were a frustration that would not be tolerated for long. Such a dog would be given away. A cat lover Jim was not, for felines were too independant and could not be persuaded to hop onto the back of a truck.

He raised birds of many kinds, Jim especially liked waterfowl. Maybe it was the vibrant colour of the males or the flat bills that gave them a look of self-confidence. With the Massey-Ferguson front-end loader, Jim scraped down into the earth at a low spot in the backyard of the Townline property. He hit the water table and scooped out enough soil to make a permanent duck pond. Next, he purchased three Graylag Geese which were free to roam the backyard and splash in the pond at their will. The gander was a fearsome brute who would bend down his neck, arch up his head, hiss, and threaten to bite anyone that came close to his beloved ladies.

The young boys were terrified and named the beast "Gray Fatty Boy." One day James and Harry were playing on the lawn in the backyard when Gray Fatty Boy spied the boys then rapidly waddled towards them in a charge. Five-year-old Harry turned to run but the gander running with wings flapping was on him in seconds. With its formidable vice-like mandibles, it clamped onto the skin on Harry's back. Harry screamed, got the goose off, and ran sobbing into the house. Mother pulled off his shirt exposing a reddened welt.

After that encounter, the boys steered clear of the geese. Cleopatra, the German Pointer had her spot in the backyard, chained to a doghouse. The boys would sometimes play with the friendly pooch and would climb onto the doghouse. On one occasion as the dog lay resting, Gray Fatty Boy ventured over emitting its nasty hiss and perhaps trying to get another nip of young boy flesh. Cleopatra lay motionless, raised her head, then bolted. The gander had come within range of the chain. The dog jumped up in a flash, latching its jaws onto the side of the fat bird. Gray Fatty Boy flapped frantically and managed to free itself from the canine's jaws, but it was not unscathed. A patch of feathers had been torn out revealing a gaping open wound on the goose's side. Within days it was clear that the unwary goose was suffering from the discoloured festering sore. It was not going to heal so Jim put the once majestic goose out of its misery.

Jim added to his waterfowl collection, purchasing a selection of ducks at the Stouffville Flea Market. He acquired Mallards, Muscovies, and a peculiar upright standing duck known as Indian Runners. They were released into a fenced pen around the pond. The ducks were thriving; they were well fed on grains and had become quite tame. One morning in the spring of 1970, Jim went to the pen to fill the feeding trays as always.

"What the hell?" he exclaimed.

He was appalled at what he saw. Half of the ducks lay flat out, haphazardly scattered about the pen. Their heads had been chewed off, but the rest of their bodies had not been touched.

"What kind of beast would do such a thing?"

A cackling ruckus coming from the backyard woke Jim late the next night. James heard it too. Both jumped out of bed, charged downstairs in their pyjamas, and raced out to the duck pen. In the corner of the cage sat the masked, beady-eyed culprit with another fowl in its grip, it was a massive raccoon. Jim grabbed an iron T-bar that was leaning against the cage, headed straight for the beast, and jabbed its fat furry belly, pinning it into the corner. The raccoon hissed and spat.

"Grab the hammer by the door and bring it to me," he ordered James.

Although there were guns in the house, that bit of information somehow escaped Jim. James handed the tool to his father. Pressing on the T-bar with his left hand, he swung the hammer with his right, pelting the animal's head repeatedly in rapid succession. He pulled back the T-bar then the bulky beast plopped to the ground, lifeless. They had saved the rest of the ducks.

Nothing thrilled Jim more than to see some of his ducks and geese sitting on a clutch of eggs in a quiet corner of the pen. He would check on their nests daily when it came close to hatching time. Sometimes he would reach his hand under a brooding goose to count the eggs. She did not like it but tolerated the gentle unflinching hand. Eggs would start peeping before they hatched, then a pink beak would break a hole into the calcium shell, eventually it would peck its way out. Most of the eggs had hatched into downy yellow goslings within a day or so. Jim was delighted, taking pride as if he had helped in the incubation.

In later years Jim did incubate eggs, but not by sitting on them. Canada Geese, one of his faves, had become a very common nesting bird in the area. The birds were so big, bold, and conspicuous, that their nests could be found without much difficulty in early spring. After all, Jim was a seasoned egg hunter, so he knew where to look. He took a few eggs from one nest, then a few more from another, and maybe some from a third.

"There were still eggs left in the nest and besides, the females could lay more", he reasoned.

He took the precious cargo home, then carefully placed them in an electric incubator set to the appropriate temperature. He would look in a couple of times a day, and after a few weeks, fluffy peeping goslings pushed their way out of their shelled confinement.

Jim showing a gosling to his grandson Liam.

Waterfowl are precocial, meaning that they can walk, swim, and feed without assistance soon after hatching. Consequently, little care was required in raising the goslings. After keeping them in an enclosure for a few days, Jim liberated the yellow powder puffs into the fenced-in pond, with the other ducks and geese. The Canadas developed rapidly turning from bright yellow to dull, then to dirty gray, and finally sporting the diagnostic white cheek contrasting the black head and neck. These geese became very tame, running up to Jim whenever he called out "poulet, poulet, poulet" and came to feed them. By late summer the geese would fly away, coaxed into freedom by wild geese winging overhead. Next spring Jim would do it over again.

Birds often had the run of the place. At the Townline home, a cluster of Bantam chickens roamed the yard at will. The white rooster was small but loud and fearless. The sons named him 'Sampson' after the mighty biblical character. If anyone got close to the hens, Sampson would charge. Jim loved their presence, but he generally did not get sentimental about his birds. One evening as the family was enjoying a fine chicken dinner, Jim revealed that they were eating Sampson. James, Harry, and Ted could eat no more.

Jim would come to acquire more exotic types of pets over the years. Guinea hens with their raucous clucks, and peacocks strutted the yard. The male peacock, seeing his reflection in the basement window, would gaze into the glass admiringly, seeming to be awestruck by his own beautiful image. Then Jim bought a couple of rheas, large flightless birds native to the South American Pampas. These he kept near the garden centre, to the entertainment of customers.

Corry did not share his love of animals. She was indifferent to the strange sounds and quirky movements of birds and beasts and didn't much appreciate the fact that animals would defecate wherever they were, on the lawn, patio, or even windowsills. But she did not have much to say in the matter.

At the Millbrook farm, otherwise known as the 'Power Property', Jim installed two-metre-high wire fencing around a one-hectare portion of his property creating a paddock for his most ambitious animal adventure, deer ranching. He acquired two dozen European Red Deer in the late 1980s, which for most of the year frolicked about the pen, grazed on grass, and bred. The herd soon increased to about forty animals. These were hardly pets that Jim could play with, but instead they were part of a business venture. In spring, the antlers of males grew rapidly, full of blood vessels and covered in a soft living velvet. At this stage, the animals were corralled and sedated. Antlers were removed by a veterinarian following strict protocols. The tender material was delicately packed then shipped to Asia to be used in tradi-

Jim with one of his Red Deer at the feeding trough.

tional Chinese medicine. Deer were part of the menagerie for about ten years before Jim sold off the herd and dismantled the pens.

Jim also raised some scaly cold-blooded animals, and these weren't exactly pets either. A four-metre-deep pond was excavated out of a wet depression at the back corner of the Taunton property in 1971. It was spring fed and therefore cool enough to stock with rainbow trout. Jim obtained 100 mid-sized fish for release. The fish seemed to fare well in the confined waters. They grew well on pelletized fish food that they were fed daily. Jim or visitors would occasionally cast in a line and catch a fish. Jim could now fish on his own property.

In the sunny days of summer, however, large mats of algae formed on the pond surface, an indication of high nutrients and stagnant conditions. As the algae decayed the pondwater would be robbed of its oxygen which the trout depended on to survive. The fish had to stay in the deeper colder water. Jim was told that copper sulphate could be used to control algae without harming the fish. In fact, copper sulphate is toxic at higher concentrations.

James was assigned the weekly job of algae control. He would place an amount of blue crystals in a burlap rag tied on the end of a stick, then walk around the pond rim, swishing the rag in the water until all of the copper sulphate had dissolved. Jim would say "make sure you use enough" and then indicated the amount he thought should be used. James took a conservative approach, using about one-third the amount that his father recommended. It worked well, the algae disappeared, and the water cleared. One week, James was away so Jim did the job himself. He assumed that if a little was good, then more would be better. It wasn't. A couple of days later, many of the fish were floating belly up on the surface. Jim had applied too much algae killer which also killed the fish!

A few years later Jim stocked the pond with largemouth bass, better suited to the warm water conditions than trout. They even made well defended nests in the shallows producing many little bass. Bass are voracious predators, however. Before long they had eaten all the tadpoles, frogs, and minnows in the pond. With nothing else to eat, the large bass gobbled up all the baby bass until only a couple large ones remained. They continued to feed opportunistically on whatever might venture into the pond.

CHAPTER 29

Exotic Travels in the 1980s and Beyond

The world so fascinated Jim and he wanted to see as much of it as he could. He would make many brief forays to exotic lands with Corry by his side. Acquiring a level of wealth gave them the ability to experience some of the amazing places of the planet in relative comfort. They had stayed at all-inclusive Caribbean resorts, signed up for guided bus tours, and luxurious ocean cruises, but they also enjoyed independent travels where itineraries were less predictable, and the unexpected could happen. Such trips were the most memorable. Corry may have had higher standards for comfort than Jim, but she too was game for adventure.

In the winter of 1981, Jim and Corry drove a light pickup truck equipped with a camper on back for a month through central Mexico. A bit risky, perhaps, but Corry had faith that Jim could get them through just about anything with his positive, self-assured attitude. Their Spanish was rudimentary. They barely understood the locals' response when asking directions. Road signs were minimal and often unclear. Nevertheless, hand gestures and patience went a long way, and with whatever maps were available they motored their way through winding mountain roads and narrow cobblestone streets without mishap. They visited historic towns, sprawling markets, and passed through breathtaking landscapes ranging from desert to tropical forest. They would overnight in private campgrounds whenever they could, for these were the safest. Otherwise, they made do with whatever was available.

Sometimes they asked a poor campesino if they could park on his land for a night. One evening they drove the pickup onto the sand of a secluded beach to camp. Jim thought that they should be safe here. Arguing gruff voices woke them in the middle of the night. Were these banditos coming to rob them? No place to hide now! Jim opened the door cautiously and looked out on a group of rowdy fishermen pursuing their quarry along the shore. The men politely moved off once they saw the gringo campers.

In the morning, Jim discovered that parking in dry sand was not such a good idea. They could get no traction in the unconsolidated substrate. Spinning tires just dug the truck deeper. Just as in snow, Jim knew that the trick was to jack up the back wheels then put branches, boards, garbage, and whatever material was at hand under the tires to get enough traction to get them out.

They had pre-arranged to pick up James and Ted at the airport in the Pacific resort town of Puerto Vallarta so that the boys could spend a week with them. It was their Christmas present. All four crowded into the front seat of the pickup for a Mexican road trip. Kamstras did not lie on a beach at some plush resort for a week. No, they made tracks. The men took turns at the wheel, driving a great circle that brought them to Manzanillo, Guadalajara, Tepic, and back to Puerto Vallarta. The loaded pickup struggled up winding switchbacks to cross mountain passes, and across broad plains of mesquite. They explored uninhabited coastlines, went body surfing, sampled unfamiliar foods, strolled through crowded markets, and sampled tequila at the factory where it was made. Jim knew much about the *artesanía* from his previous years' experience, so he led them to various market stalls. He had no thoughts of importing more of this stuff, however. There was still plenty in the store back home. James and Ted were dropped off at the airport in PV, then Jim and Corry continued on for a couple more weeks.

Jim, Ted, Corry and James with the camper in Guadalajara, Mexico.

In January 1982 Jim and Corry were again driving south in the blue pickup but they would go even further. James and his colleague Joe Fragoso had travelled to Belize, planning to stay the better part of a year to study the ecology of a large mammal known as the Baird's Tapir. They were students in the biology program at Trent University engaged in field research for their theses. The parents were going to visit their son. What better excuse for an exotic road trip to Central America? The camper was loaded with food, clothing and supplies they would need for the long journey. Jim had also purchased a used 100 cc motorbike to take down to James, which he locked up in the camper. They cruised across the US in three days, then followed less direct roads along the Mexican Gulf coast to the Yucatan Peninsula. Whenever they stopped in a campground, Jim had first to pull out the motorcycle to be able to use the camper. The bike attracted a lot of attention among young Mexican men, many who made offers to buy it. Jim made sure to chain and lock it securely.

Paul and Gina had flown down to Cancun to join them on this expedition. With four adults pressed together in the front cab, they crossed into Belize. The former British colony was more rustic and backward than they expected. There were no campgrounds to be found so they parked for the night on whatever quiet patch of vacant ground they could. No problem since the camper was a self-sufficient unit complete with a stove, food, water, and sleeping quarters.

Belize had an uneasy feeling about it, however. It was poor with dilapidated buildings and suspicious-looking characters just hanging around whenever they stopped. Jim had no qualms about approaching strangers and could easily start up a conversation. At least they spoke English in this country. Paul was equally forthright with the locals. Both being businessmen, they would enquire about the local economy, what work they did, and what living conditions were like. Thus, they learned about life in Belize.

The camper left the main Western Highway, then bumped along rutted dirt roads to get to the remote village of Augustine where James resided. The vehicle pulled up to a wooden shack on stilts. James sat on the step with his girlfriend, Sue, then looked up in surprise. A joyous reunion for James with his folks, he had been away for a month by then. The parents brought a wealth of food: steaks, fresh produce, and desserts, so all enjoyed the barbeque that night. Since there was no functional electricity or refrigeration in the village,

James' food options were limited to rice and beans, canned goods, locally grown vegetables and salted pigtails. Corry worried that her normally skinny son was losing even more weight on such a deficient diet. Jim took out the motorcycle and instructed James on its operation.

James led his relatives for a hike around his remote study area, which involved climbing through a high ceiling limestone cave and wading through a jungle stream looking for tapir tracks along sandbars. Jim could not appreciate what James was doing in this poor excuse of an uncivilized country.

"Why would James come to this God-forsaken place to study an animal that no one cares about when he can have it all at home?" Jim asked Joe Fragoso when the two were conversing.

Nevertheless, Jim accepted that his son was doing what he wanted. Jim would fully support him if that was what he wanted to do.

Jim wanted to see the spectacular and famous Mayan ruins of Tikal since these were not far away in the neighbouring country of Guatemala. With James, Joe, and Sue riding in the camper, and the others up front, the pickup made its way through the ramshackle border crossing at Melchor de Mencos. Not far into Guatemala, the vehicle was stopped at a military checkpoint just beyond the village. Two uniformed soldiers holding semi-automatic rifles and speaking in Spanish, ordered everyone out of the vehicle. Joe, with his Portuguese background, was fluent so he could translate.

The soldiers were mestizo, no more than 17 or 18 years of age and probably illiterate. They searched under the seat, then into the camper opening cabinets and looking under the beds. Paul had a large roll of American bills, several hundred dollars' worth, sitting in a cup in a cupboard. It seemed like a safe enough spot when he put it there. He was sweating now. If these rifle-toting adolescents noticed such cash, they would likely take it. Luckily the soldiers were not so observant. Instead, they found and confiscated two decks of playing cards. The youths would now have something to do in their lonely outpost. They gestured for the party to carry on.

Although only a hundred kilometres to Flores, the dirt road was so rutted and potholed that the camper had to take its time, taking three hours to get there. It was late afternoon when they reached that town, but they could find no secure place to park for the night. Jim drove away from town then followed a backroad that headed towards Lake Peten Itza. The lakeshore was deserted except for a single thatch hut, home to a suspicious family of campesinos. It was not an ideal place to spend the night, but the sun was setting, and they were running out of options. Joe translated for Jim, asking the head of the household if they could camp overnight. Jim handed the man a few quetzal notes. He held up his hands, not wanting any payment, but Jim insisted. Next day they reached Tikal. Ancient pyramidal temples rose above the tall jungle canopy, while howler monkeys bellowed from the nearby forest. The setting was idyllic, certainly worth the trip, but they could not stay long. The Guatemalan visa only allowed the truck to stay for two days in the country. They bumped their way back to the Belize border on those horrible, rutted tracks that passed for roads in the Petén.

Before entering Guatemala, they heard rumours of military-guerrilla confrontations, but Jim thought such stories exaggerated. Actually, the early 1980s were a particularly tense time in Guatemala, a country known for repressive regimes, gross human rights violations, and guerilla insurgency. If Jim had read the headlines, he would never have driven his personal vehicle into that precarious country. He may have been a risk-taker, but he wasn't crazy. They saw no other North American cars on the Guatemalan roads, probably because other would-be tourists had read the headlines.

Returning to Belize, they headed to Ambergris Caye for some coastal relaxation and fishing before the long drive back north. After dropping off Paul and Gina at the Cancun airport, Corry suggested taking their time on the return drive through Mexico, stopping at some ancient ruins, historic towns, and landmarks along the way.

"I think we've been on the road long enough, Corry," Jim explained directly.

Disappointed, Corry knew her man, and when his mind was made up. The drive back home was a blur. Early breakfast, then long hours of motoring the most direct highways making only brief stops for meals and washroom breaks. For future travels, Corry would do her best to convince Jim to book a scheduled flight instead of driving. Then Jim would not be able to shorten their vacation plan.

By the mid 1990s, Jim and Corry were making about three overseas forays per year. Many were organized tours with pre-arranged itineraries that guarantee visits the must-see sites. Tours take care of booking hassles and provide greater safety, especially in country's with crime-ridden urban areas and language barriers. By this stage of life, they were getting more cautious about travelling on their own in Third World countries, at least most of the time. Even organized tours are not entirely free from mishaps, however.

Africa, known for its diversity of large mammals on the open savannah, was on Jim's list of places to see. They booked onto a wildlife safari to Kenya and Tanzania in February of 1990. They were shuffled around in a van with a small group of tourists that sped across dusty tracks through a range of parks, including Amboseli, Masai Mara, Ngorongoro Crater, and the Serengeti. Their savanna-seasoned driver and guide was intimately familiar with what looked like monotonous terrain. He knew just where the spectacular beasts that they had come to see would be hanging out. Close encounters with elephants, lions, crocodiles, leopards, and water buffalo rewarded the group, all from the safety of their van, of course.

The van drove along a main road through the open plains. It suddenly jerked to a stop, with the engine revving madly under the hood. The driver shook his head and threw up his arms, then shut off the engine. He went outside to open the hood and see what the matter was. Jim went over to look as well since he had some idea of mechanics. The fan belt had broken, and the driver had no spare. Jim had been confronted with this issue before, and he had an idea.

"Do any of the ladies happen to have a pair of nylon pantyhose in your suitcases?" Jim asked the group.

One woman did, so she retrieved them and handed it to the driver. The driver took the pantyhose, cut it up, and tried to tie the ends of the broken fan belt together.

"No, no, no!" Jim cried out. "That will never work. You need to wrap the nylon around the flywheels then tie the ends together for a makeshift belt."

It was too late; the hosiery was in pieces and now useless. Another tourist looked at Jim and shrugged. "They just want to figure it out for themselves," he said. "No point in interfering." The driver radioed their lodge to notify them of the breakdown. The sweating tourists endured the blistering sun for hours before another van showed up to return them to the lodge.

Jim having a discussion with van drivers in Kenya.

In the winter of 1992, Jim and Corry joined a group of a dozen Ontario farmers on an organized tour around New Zealand. A bus driven by the amiable Kiwi guide, Athole Bennie, ferried the group around North and South Island. Athole was the perfect host for such a group. Not only was he a farmer himself, but also a former national champion of the New Zealand Ploughing Match. The tour took in many of the sites of the southern nation, often focusing on features of agricultural interest.

Each night all of the participants stayed in the homes of affluent farmers instead of hotels. Athole gave a running commentary of sites they passed along the way while keeping both hands on the wheel as the bus moved through the undulating landscape. Almost everywhere they went, he would relay tales of farmers that he knew, their mishaps, of fortunes made or strange events.

At one point, Athole stopped the bus seeing a sheep in the pasture, lying flat on its back with its four legs pointing straight up, as if in rigour mortis.

He looked at Jim and instructed, "Walk down in the pasture there and give that old ewe a kick, firm but not too hard?".

Jim marched over, then kicked the side of the rotund woolly animal. It rolled onto its side, stood up, bleated furiously, then trotted away.

Athole explained, "Don't know why, but sometimes a sheep like that falls over and cannot get up on its own. It just needs a little push".

A day or so later, Jim and Corry sat together in the seat just behind the driver. The bus was descending a hill when Corry noticed something.

"Jim, the driver, something is wrong!".

Athole was slumping over, and the bus was starting to veer off the road. Jim reacted in a flash. He hopped out of his seat, grabbed the steering wheel, and pushed Athole's sagging body aside so he could get in the driver's seat. With one foot on the brakes and the other on the clutch, Jim eased the bus over to the roadside, bringing it to a safe stop, then he shut off the engine.

All the passengers could see what was happening and were soon aware of how narrowly they avoided disaster. Jim was an instant hero. He may well have saved many lives or, at the very least, prevented crippling injuries. Athole regained consciousness in a dazed state after a few moments and the company sent another driver to replace him, but not for long. Two days later, Athole was back behind the wheel as if nothing happened, entertaining the group with his tales again.

The South American country of Ecuador seemed safe enough so they arranged a flight there in January 1993. Part of this trip entailed a pre-arranged week onboard a floating hotel on the Rio Napo, a tributary of the Amazon in the eastern lowlands. They also decided on spending another week on their own exploring the picturesque landscape of the High Andes on their own. The plane's loudspeaker announced that they would be momentarily landing in Ecuador, then touched down. Jim and Corry deboarded, had their passports stamped at customs, then waited at the baggage carousel for their luggage. It never appeared. They enquired with airport staff, then learned that they were in Guayaquil, not Quito, their intended destination. The plane had gone on with their luggage, however. Not a big deal, they found a hotel at the airport, then airline staff rebooked them on a Quito bound flight next morning.

Corry felt dizzy and nauseated within a few hours after they arrived in the 3000-metre-high city of Quito. When Jim drove their rental vehicle higher into the mountains, Corry felt even worse and started vomiting. It must be altitude sickness they decided, her body had developed a strong reaction to the thin air of high elevation, but she had never suffered from this before. Jim looked over his road map and tried to avoid roads that took them over mountain passes, but even the Central Valley wedged between the eastern and western ranges of the Andes was still as high as Denver. Following highways with few guiding road signs and small-scaled maps made navigating a challenge. As they proceeded southward, the land sloped downward, and Corry started feeling better. Now she could enjoy the panpipes and charangos so characteristic of the Andean folkloric music. Thankfully, their second week aboard the steamy floating hotel was in the Amazon lowlands.

The experience of visiting a foreign land is enhanced when there is a close personal connection with someone from there. So thought Jim when his Jamaican friend, Gilbert (not his real name), invited the Kamstras to join him on a trip to his homeland over New Year's 1996. Gilbert was a jovial chap who had lived in Peterborough for several years but frequently returned to Jamaica, where he had many friends and relatives. Gilbert occasionally dropped in on Jim and Corry at the Millbrook farm, sometimes stayed over for supper, and the Kamstras had also been to his place to socialize. Airline tickets were purchased in anticipation.

Gilbert, along with his lady friend, drove the four of them to the Toronto airport to catch the Jamaica bound jet. Gilbert owned a vehicle on the island, so also did the driving while there. They had spent a couple of days together touring, then Gilbert had arranged for them to stay overnight at a shabby establishment owned by one of his friends. Corry could put up with rustic, but this place was a dump. She was not impressed: unkempt grounds, garbage, chickens running about, and even their room was not clean. They weren't even near a beach, for which Jamaica is so famous.

Gilbert took Jim and Corry to a place of better lodging. He said that he needed to attend to some family matters for a day and overnight, promising to return to pick them up to visit other places. Jim and Corry waited at the hotel. Gilbert did not appear the day and time that he said he would. They started to worry. They had no phone or way of contacting the man. Was he going to show up, had he been in an accident? After another day and still no sign, it was apparent

Corry and Jim on deck of a cruise ship.

that Gilbert was not coming. A hired taxi drove Jim and Corry to the airport at the end of their stay.

There was Gilbert with his lady in the terminal. He would barely acknowledge their presence. When Jim approached him, Gilbert grumbled something about Jim taking off on them? Was there some misunderstanding about where and when they would meet? Was Gilbert offended by some negative comments they made about his friend's accommodation? Gilbert would not talk so Jim never learned why the old Jamaican neglected to come back for them. Once in Toronto, Gilbert rushed off without the Kamstras, but he had their winter coats in his car, and it was a cold January day. Jim and Corry found another way home. Months later, Gilbert stopped in at their house to return the jackets, but he did not stick around long enough to explain himself. That was one Caribbean vacation they were happy to forget.

Joking with a local in Barbados.

A year later, they were again bound for the West Indies, but this would be a very different trip. On New Years' day 1997, the Kamstras along with Paul and Gina were strapped into the seats of Jim's noisy Cessna, bound for the Bahamas. They had only been airborne for a few minutes, but Jim, as the responsible pilot, felt uneasy. Snow was coming down through a low cloud ceiling, and the forecast was questionable. No point in pushing it. Jim turned the plane around and returned to Oshawa airport.

Five days later, the sky was clear enough to leave. They were able to take off but only made about 200 kilometres to Dunkirk, New York, before low cloud banks and snow forced them down again. Winter flying in a small plane is subject to the whims of the weather. If it took five days to reach the Bahamas, then that is what it took. They were heading out to a rented house on the island of Eleuthera for a month. If they arrived a few days late, it was no big deal. Jim was in his winter, non-work mode. He was calm and contented to be flying his own plane. They enjoyed their time dining, fishing, socializing and swimming on the carefree Eleuthera. The Cessna also allowed them to visit many of the coralline out islands since most had landing strips.

Costa Rica called in January of 2003. Jim and Corry rented a cottage on the northeast coast for a couple of weeks. James, Lynda, and their three-and-a-half-year-old son, Nathan, flew down for a week. As usual, Jim had planned a varied itinerary for these days: swimming on the beach, trails at Santa Rosa National Park, take part in a small-town rodeo at the village of Santa Cruz, and a drive up to the Arenal Volcano.

Jim had rented a small standard car, a pretty basic model but apparently dependable and just big enough that the five of them could squeeze in. The tires were very worn, almost bald, and low in air pressure. Jim pulled over at a local gas station. He found a functioning air hose along the wall of the station, which lacked a pressure gauge. Not to worry, Jim pumped in air until the tires were what he thought to be just firm enough. With all aboard, Jim drove the windy and often pot-holed roads into the verdant mountainous interior.

While driving along, they heard a pop at the front right, then the vehicle suddenly started vibrating, accompanied by a rapid loud flapping.

"What the heck?" Jim pulled the car over, coming to a complete stop.

They inspected the front right tire. It wasn't flat, but a flap of rubber had detached from the tire tread, such that it slapped the pavement with every rotation of the wheel. They could not drive on very far like this, so Jim drove the limping vehicle to the nearest gas station where they had the unusable tire changed, then back on the road.

Within twenty minutes, the car started shaking again, this time with loud, rapid flapping coming from the front left. A flap of rubber detached from the other front tire. They needed another garage, but this time there were no more spares.

The grease-stained mechanic took one look at the tire, nodded his head and said, "*demasiada presion de aire.*" Too much air pressure. Jim had unknowingly over-pumped the nearly treadless tires, which in combination with velocity on hot rutted roads, caused the rubber to split off in strips. Jim had no choice but to purchase a new tire if he wanted to drive the jalopy back to the cottage.

Jim and Corry tried a different kind of Costa Rican trip in January 2007, as volunteers for Habitat for Humanity, a global non-governmental organization that builds and provides homes for underprivileged families. At their fiftieth wedding anniversary celebration in the previous September, the Kamstras asked that guests make a donation to Habitat in lieu of a gift. Over $5000 was thus raised for the cause.

They joined a group of about a dozen other Canadians in constructing a house in a small village. Work entailed bricklaying, framing, hanging doors, laying tiles, and carpentry. Corry, who was not skilled at carpentry, did her part straightening nails in the hot sun. Jim found that many of the volunteers were unaccustomed to this type of work and that the rate of progress was not very efficient. Since this was not his project and he was only here for a short spell, he decided not to say too much. He enjoyed the experience and the passion of the other volunteers in helping someone less fortunate.

They booked a river cruise in Russia that took them on the Volga River from St. Petersburg to Moscow and liked it so much that they purchased passage on many ship cruises over the coming years. In autumn 2004, Jim and Corry boarded a cruise ship in Fort Lauderdale that ended in Cape Town, South Africa, with stops in Trinidad, French Guiana, Brazil, Senegal, Ghana, Togo, and Namibia.

A few years later, they embarked on an even longer cruise that spanned much of the South Pacific, starting at Valparaiso, Chile ending in Aukland, New Zealand. They climbed aboard the MV Discovery, the very same ship that appeared in the 1970s television series, *The Love Boat*. That ship took them to a smattering of South Seas nations, including Pitcairn Island, Easter Island, Bora Bora, Tahiti, Fiji, Tonga, and Rarotonga in the Cook Islands. Despite the onboard lectures, casinos, and nightly entertainment, the long days at sea were too much for the restless man. Jim could only circle the deck so many times looking out on the often-featureless horizon before boredom set in.

Since it was decades since Jim and Corry vacationed with all of their three sons, they decided to treat them along with their spouses and children to a week-long Caribbean Cruise. They all flew into San Juan, Puerto Rico, on the very last day of 2011 to board the Celebrity Summit Cruise. Jim was a seasoned cruiser, so he knew the gimmicks.

"Don't sign up for the ship's excursions, or fall for their warnings of safety," Jim advised. "They are overpriced, crowded and will only just take you to the tourist traps. You can always find a taxi who will take you to more interesting spots, on your schedule, and at a better price."

In Barbados, their first port of call, Jim had an excellent local contact. Ian Lowe spent summers working on a nearby fruit farm but

Kamstras on the Caribbean Cruise over New Years 2012 . Back row: James, Ted, Harry, Jim. Front row: Debbie, Liam, Corry, Nathan and Lynda.

returned each winter to his balmy native homeland. Ian had befriended the Kamstras and had frequently visited them at their home. He was thrilled to now be able to show off his island to Jim's family. Jim had arranged to meet him when the ship docked at the harbour in Bridgetown. There was Ian, all smiles, so happy to show the Kamstras around his island.

From a seedy pool hall, the historic cathedral, and to a nature reserve overrun with exotic monkeys, this was the real Barbados. On St. Kitts, Jim worked out a deal with a friendly, but insightful, taxi driver named Eddy Winston. He then summoned the family to climb into the van for an intimate island tour. Eddy knew his island inside and took them into areas rarely frequented by tourists, including to a simple out of the way village to the home his elderly grandmother. Jim was right about avoiding the tours offered by the cruise boat.

Corry and Jim would continue travelling each year to many more destinations for as long as they were able. Jim visited sixty countries over his lifetime. The Caribbean cruise would be the last trip that Jim's nuclear family would take together, however.

Corry and Jim did many trips together by air, land and water.

CHAPTER 30

One More Dream Home

Between the ever-increasing traffic on Taunton Road and lack of privacy, Jim and Corry tired of the 1470 Taunton Road home beside Kamstra Landscaping. With Harry now in charge of running the garden centre, it made sense for him to live on the premises and keep an eye on the shop instead of his parents.

Jim searched through the local real estate listings where he found a 30-hectare piece of turf that just might be the thing. Situated on Concession Road 3 west of Newcastle, it bordered a stretch of Wilmott Creek, renowned for its spring run of rainbow trout and autumn run of Chinook salmon. Major fish passage across his very own property—now that was special! Most of the land was open cropland, growing corn at the time, but it also had a small orchard producing a good crop of apples and pears. A small ravine with a tributary of the Wilmott flowed eastward, bisecting the farm. It had an on-line pond held back by an earthen dam crossed by a rickety bridge. In the middle, a tree-lined laneway led to a stately old two-story farmhouse that had seen better days and was rented out. Behind it stood a large shed and wooden barn with a silo. The property was perfect as far as Jim was concerned.

Corry had a different idea. She was not really a country girl to start with, and now in their late sixties, she preferred to be closer to town, not further out. She thought that being so far from Oshawa isolated them from their less mobile ageing friends. Like usual, Jim got his way. He put in an offer and the seller accepted; the property was theirs.

They considered renovating the old farmhouse but thought it would be a finicky project with unforeseen issues that would be as costly as building a new one. Instead, they hired an architect to come up with a novel house design that would incorporate their own specifications at the west end of the property. Work started almost immediately. This time contactors completed all of the construction. The 2500 square foot brick bungalow was not excessively large for a country estate, but spacious enough for the two of them, and to entertain family and friends. When the furnished house was decorated with her personal touch, it became Corry's cherished home as well. They moved in early spring 1998 to the new address: 3225 Concession Road 3, Newcastle.

The Newcastle house under construction.

Jim put up a shed and coop to keep a few chickens, and he fenced in the pond to contain ducks and Canada Geese. He had the yard tastefully landscaped with a variety of coniferous and deciduous trees and shrubs. His green thumb shined in the vegetable garden that produced a great bounty and variety by late summer to which he generously shared with family members. Flowering plants in a plethora of form and colours filled the beds around the house. Having the Dutch mentality of land management, Jim always had much to keep himself busy.

"It's a lot of work when you own property."

He cut down dead trees, regularly mowed unused open areas of the floodplain, and created a network of trails, making most of the land accessible to his golf cart. Even at 84 years of age, he was still cutting down trees with a long-bladed chain saw, just as he had as a young man.

About two-thirds of the property was arable and under cultivation. That portion had been leased to a local fruit farmer to grow corn or soybeans. It was a common practice for owners of large rural properties to rent out a large portion of their land to a contract farmer who would grow and harvest cash crops. The amount of rent paid by the farmer was minuscule, but this practice significantly reduced the land taxes by putting it into the low agricultural rate.

A couple of years after purchasing the land, Dave Gibson, the neighbouring fruit farmer, rented the arable portion from Jim, then transformed the cornfields into strawberry fields. That was fine. The rent was still a pittance, but at least the Kamstras could have all the strawberries they ever wanted. The family came for a strawberry picking gathering and feast each year in the berry season. Some years later, Gibson plowed under the strawberries and turned the land back into growing cereal crops.

His relationship with brother Harmen had been on Jim's mind for some time. They had become estranged and had barely spoken for years. They would cross paths at weddings or funerals but avoided each other. Both could be outspoken and bull-headed, so Jim had a roller-coaster relationship with his older brother. Only two years apart in age, they grew up together and were very close throughout their youth. They commiserated over the wrath of their father. They played, explored and engaged in so many activities together. They reunited in Nova Scotia, frequently associating to fish. Later in Ontario, a rift developed between them. It may have started with Jim's annoyance that Harmen had abandoned his family. Harmen may have been jealous of Jim's success in business and prosperity.

As the two were now well into their senior years, Jim realized how silly it was for brothers to live so close yet have no interaction. He called up Harmen and invited him to come out for a coffee along with Sid. That's all it took, one reaching out to the other. Harmen came out to join them. He was grayer and stooped over a little, but still full of stories. There was much to talk about, so many memories as well as more recent experiences. The three Kamstras agreed to meet at a Tim Horton's Donut shop weekly whenever they could. They continued with this new brotherly tradition until it no longer became physically possible for them to do so.

The three brothers: Harmen, Sid and Jim in 2010.

CHAPTER 31

A Stroke of Bad Luck

On his 85th birthday in May 2015, Jim appeared to be as healthy as ever and continued to lead a full active life. Corry, his sons, their spouses, and grandchildren celebrated this milestone birthday with him at an Oshawa restaurant. Birthdays were special to Jim; he loved to be the centre of attention as friends and family surrounded him. At a time of life when nearly all his acquaintances were retired, Jim had no such plans. Working the soil at Kamstra Landscaping gave him purpose and kept him in "the game." And there were so many places that he still wanted to see. Summer arrived for Jim just as it had in previous years. Along with Corry, they mixed their time between work, gardening, and leisure at home, with the occasional excursion away.

Jim celebrating his 85th birthday.

In late August, Jim and Corry took a break from work to spend a little time driving around the scenic Finger Lakes in New York state. They had scheduled four days away, but Jim suddenly wanted to return home after only two. It wasn't the first time that he had cut a road trip short, so Corry, a little disappointed, succumbed to his wish.

"Corry, you do the driving," he instructed.

This was uncharacteristic; they always split the driving on a long trip. Was Jim feeling alright? If not, he did not say. Corry drove through Canadian customs then continued on the final stretch home, while Jim sat uncharacteristically quiet in his seat.

Two days later, on September 1st, Jim drove his Toyota car along familiar streets. He was thinking about flying. Ever since he sold the Cessna CF-ZKO a year earlier, Jim was itching to get back into the pilot seat. He stopped into the Oshawa Airport to find out about a used aircraft that he was thinking of purchasing to co-own with Harry. He returned to Kamstra Landscaping a little later.

Driving up the incline of Taunton Road, he slowed down the car as he was about to turn into the garden centre parking lot. Something was wrong with the vehicle. The steering wheel was pulling to one side. He just managed to turn into the yard when he had a strange sensation. It wasn't the vehicle. Something was wrong with him! His whole left side would not do what he commanded; it felt paralyzed. He was able to drive into the yard, making a wide arc. Matt Smith, a worker who was moving some plants in the garden centre, looked up at the passing car.

Strange that Jim seemed to be leaning over while driving peculiarly, Matt thought, but he went back to his task.

The vehicle ground to a halt. Jim reached around with his right hand and barely managed to open the door, then just slid out onto the ground. He tried to call out for help, but no one heard. He pulled up his right leg, got his foot onto the steering wheel and forced it down on the horn. Debbie, who was in the office, heard the continuous horn blast from the parking area and came out running. Jim was lying on the ground, legs up in the car seat. His face looked off somehow. The mouth drooped down to the left, and he was slurring words. Debbie could see the helpless terror in his eyes. She punched in 911 on her cell phone, then tried to move him into a more comfortable position. He was dead weight, so instead, Debbie placed a rolled jacket under his neck and waited.

An ambulance arrived in minutes. Two medics, a man and woman, gave Jim a quick on the spot examination. After questioning Debbie about what happened, they gently hoisted him onto a stretcher, into the back of the wagon and then raced off to the emergency ward at Oshawa General Hospital. Jim had suffered a stroke, and a severe one. His left side lacked any feeling or movement.

Rapid medical attention was critical. Every minute that ticks by reduces a stroke victim's ability to recover. The quick response of medical staff getting Jim to the hospital to administer vital medication and treatment likely saved his life.

Meanwhile, Debbie jumped into her car then sped to Newcastle to tell Corry in person. They drove to the hospital together, as Debbie relayed all the details. Corry was devasted and started to shake when she first saw her man, lying on the hospital bed, looking so broken. She approached him tenderly. He felt so helpless but relieved to see her.

The family was in shock. How could this happen to such a vibrant man, the head of the family? He was always so strong and in control! Jim lay in the hospital bed, semi-conscious, confused and hallucinating. The x-ray showed pooling of blood on the brain. His speech was slurred but coherent, and he knew what had happened. Thank god he was still alive!

The first weeks following a stroke are crucial for this is when most of the recovery will occur. At first, he could make no movements on the entire left side of his body. A faint tingling feeling started in a couple of days then got more intense. A few days later, he could wiggle his fingers and toes, the first hopeful sign. The ISU administered a rigorous program to get patients mobile again through physiotherapy sessions and assisted movement.

Once Jim got past the traumatic first few days, he made his mind up to get better. Whatever it took, he would do. Physiotherapy was the key to getting better so he eagerly accepted as much as the hospital would provide. He pushed himself to the point of exhaustion in the sessions. Jim was going to beat this thing, damn it! His future prognosis was heavy on his mind, however. Would he ever be able to drive again? He would just have to take one little step at a time. First, he had to learn to walk with a walker. No way was he going to be confined to a wheelchair! He did exercises during the sessions, then worked his arms and legs when alone in bed.

He requested additional exercises. Ever so slowly he was regaining movement.

Corry, the love of his life, accompanied him faithfully in the ISU for much of every day. Jim also received many visits from friends and family as word got out about his predicament. These helped to build up his spirits. Sharing the room in the bed beside him, lay Gary Hooper, a country singer who also suffered a stroke. The two formed a bond, each encouraging the other, and praising each other with each minor gain. The hospital let Jim stay for two full months, more than they allow most patients. At the end of it, Gary had made a near-complete recovery and was able to return home. Jim would not be so lucky.

By the time of his release from Oshawa General, Kamstra could move about, pushing a walker but only with assistance from others. Jim was relieved to be back in the Newcastle home with Corry, but it would never be the same. The two of them were able to get by with some incoming helpers as well as assistance by family members. Jim readily accepted whatever physiotherapy we could get in a desperate attempt to improve his physical condition.

On a warm sunny day in late April, Harry came over to clean up the grounds on the Newcastle property. After being confined inside for months, Jim relished the thought of getting out in the spring air. Harry took him for a ride on the golf cart. Despite his mobility limitations, Jim was not merely content to just go for a ride; he wanted to drive it. Reluctantly Harry let him drive while sitting close beside him. That worked okay. A little while later, Jim sat alone on the golf cart, then started driving slowly across the backyard. Harry, who was raking the lawn nearby, looked up in disbelief.

Somehow Jim moved his immobile left foot just enough to get it stuck between the gas pedal and the floor. The cart accelerated, turning into a wide arc across the lawn. Jim clung onto the steering wheel until the cart rammed into a steel animal cage on the side of the shed. He was flung off to the side, striking some object that tore open a gash on his left hand. Jim lay on the ground in a heap, groaning and complaining about the pain in his back. Harry ran over, lifted him, and carried him to the car. Corry and Debbie hopped in, as Harry drove off to the emergency ward at Bowmanville Hospital to get Jim bandaged up.

It was now apparent that Jim and Corry were unable to manage living in the Newcastle home themselves.

Although hesitant, Jim, along with Corry, was willing to try residing in a sunny west-facing apartment in White Cliffe Terrace retirement home in Courtice for a month. The month extended to two, then another, and eventually, they settled in, becoming residents. Jim continued with twice weekly physiotherapy sessions at an outside facility. No matter how hard he tried, however, he saw no further improvement.

The couple now knew they could never return to live at 3225 Concession Road 3. The large rural property with their beloved home was listed on the real estate market and sold within a month. Their lifetime of accumulated belongings had to be removed from the premises by the end of May. Jim and Corry took some of the most cherished items to the limited space in their apartment. The three sons divided the rest. Algoma Orchards, an apple growing operation that already owned hundreds of hectares in the vicinity, purchased the property. It broke Jim's heart to have to part with his personal piece of paradise and a lifetime of accumulated mementos. It just had to be done.

Amid the unhappy changes, there was a cause for celebration, a wedding in the family. Harry had proposed to Debbie years earlier, but they never got around to setting a date, but now they had a good

Jim giving heartfelt speech at Harry and Debbie's wedding.

reason to pick one. Invitations were sent out for February 25 at the Acres Restaurant in Bowmanville. Jim was in the mood for a party and a few drinks, a chance to mingle with friends and relatives. Dressed up as Jim liked to be for special events, he gave a heartfelt father of the groom speech, welcoming Debbie into the family with open arms. No one noticed the small trickle flowing down her cheek.

Jim and Corry attempted to achieve a new normal given their physical limitations. Corry was able to drive their spacious Toyota so that Jim could get out of Whitecliffe Terrace for country drives and other simple excursions. She developed a routine to get Jim in and out of the car using the walker and a modified door handle insert. They had regular visits from their sons, as well as from a few remaining friends and relatives. Jim needed to use a wheelchair more and more to be able to get around as the use of the walker was becoming more challenging. Since Jim viewed the wheelchair as sign of weakness, he would not let anyone take photos of him sitting in it.

Lynda arranged a big birthday party for her husband James, who was turning 60 in late August. She rented a hall on Scugog Island where she invited many relatives and friends, and of course James' parents. A respectable number of guests showed up to wish James well. Jim was almost like his old self, chatting and kidding with people he had not seen in a while. Nobody had any idea that it would be the last time that most of them would ever see Jim.

Back at White Cliffe Terrace, Jim's condition continued to decline to the point that he was taken to the hospital on September 10. The body that had been so strong for so long was shutting down. Jim breathed his last breath at 4:30 pm on September 18, 2017.

The funeral took place on September 22, the day that would have been Jim and Corry's 61st wedding anniversary. It was held at the 177-year-old Northcutt-Elliott Funeral Home in a historic area of Bowmanville on a warm sunny day, the kind of day Jim would have loved. Some of the memorabilia of his life were displayed in the front of the internal chapel: plaques of service, his Toastmaster trophy, plane photos, and a stainless-steel spade. Photos depicting snapshots of Jim's life at various stages circulated on a screen. Hundreds came out to pay their respects for the man who was known to so many through business, clubs, family, and friendship.

The truth is he outlived so many of his friends; there would have been hundreds more if he had died a few years earlier. Following the visitation a gathering of friends and family commemorated one man's fully lived life. Sid opened with a prayer. Eulogies were given by James, Ted Curl from Kiwanis, and the concluding remarks by Harry.

Display at Jim's funeral showing some of the tools he used in life.

CHAPTER 32
A Reflection of the Man

The words from the famous song by singer Frank Sinatra, "I Did it My Way", applies to the life of Tjebbe "Jim" Kamstra. Maybe his plans did not always work out so well, but he was never afraid to try. An internal need to be financially successful was a force within him through life. Jim had that ability to see opportunities that lay before him and he had the drive to use them to his advantage. He mostly focused on the landscaping business, but also tried other money-making ventures along the way. Some worked out and some others not so well. A true independent, he tried several business partnerships over his long career, which mostly did not work for long. He needed to be the one in control.

Jim lived life to the fullest, with Corry behind him all the way.

Jim did not like indecisiveness, no dilly-dallying or pondering over a situation for days. When faced with a new predicament, his approach was "just figure out what needs to be done, then do it." Did it always work out? No, but his perseverance usually got him through. But if his plans did not work out, he did not waste a lot of time on regrets. He either learned from his experience, or he forgot about it altogether. Whatever he did, he was fully committed to the task. Jim never sat back and let others do the work.

Jim abided by the rules where he had to, but he often ignored rules when he thought he could get away with it. He would cut corners for efficiency and wasn't always diligent about safety procedures. His ventures usually worked out, but not always, after all, Jim did suffer more than his share of accidents. Nevertheless, his resilience was enviable, Kamstra always bounced back from these mishaps, and he did not let it stop him from going again.

Beyond his financial drive, Jim was a friend to many and willing to help people in need, whether they were friends, family or strangers. Yes, Kamstra had his faults: lack of patience, opinionated, difficulty compromising, and sometimes too much focus on money. But he had so many admirable qualities: he was the life of the party and always had something interesting to say.

Corry and Jim with their three sons, their wives and four grandchildren in 2017.

Everyone's luck runs out eventually. The stroke that blindsided Jim was the one obstacle he just could not rise above. Determined as he was, Kamstra fought back with everything he had, but it would not be enough. Even his strong resolve and body had its limits.

He loved life and pretty much lived the life that he wanted. Jim enjoyed a diverse range of interests, but it seems that those that he most loved all started with "F": fishing, flying, finances, flowers, friends, fun, family, and frau (Dutch for wife).

Did he accomplish everything he wanted? After his stroke, he lamented some bygone opportunities. One never can satisfy all of their dreams and life takes many twists and turns necessitating that plans and priorities shift along the way. He made the best of it and made a lot of things better. One cannot deny that Jim lived a full and enviable life.

ACKNOWLEDGEMENTS

I am indebted to those people I interviewed who were able to provide additional information about by father's life including: Corry Kamstra, Debbie Kamstra, Harry J. Kamstra, Jimmy D.H. Kamstra, Sid Kamstra, Ted Kamstra, Andy Koziar, Lynda Supryka (nee Rundle), David Peterson, Alex Pol, Ria Stolk, Paul Ten Westeneind, and Morley Travis.

Jackie Brown provided much inspiration and encouragement about writing this memoir and she edited the manuscript in detail. Suzie Plumstead, Linda Toms and Piyushi Dhir read and provided comments on an early draft.